Dedication

This book is for everyone who has served in the U.S. Military, but especially for those who served during the Vietnam War. And, it was a war, not an intervention and not a mere conflict.

Although, some of this book is irreverent, and often critical of the U.S. Army in which I served, my respect, admiration, and reverence for those soldiers who participated in this huge shameful folly is eternal. To those men and women who gave so much, to those many whose lives have seen so much irreparable damage, I honor you. The political leaders responsible for this disaster, I do not honor.

What did we learn from this?

Vietnam Calling: It's The National Guard for Me

By: John James

Why This Book?

The U.S. military is the most powerful in the world. It was then, when I served, and still is now. Best! But, in my view, this is in spite of the irrational, bungling, counterproductive, and just plain silly rules, regulations and procedures I encountered. In all fairness, the U.S. military has improved significantly since my time served. A time when the draft was in effect.

So many "experts" have argued for years about the pros and cons of an all volunteer military, and I cannot qualify as an expert. My only expertise comes as a psychologist observing human behavior and as a participant in the military - - serving because I was drafted, and, as a consequence I scrambled around to join a National Guard unit.

I will over-simplify the "voluntary service" argument with the following: In peacetime – no draft; in wartime – draft. I know this brings up the argument of what is wartime: this is especially applicable because U.S. Presidents have circumvented the consent of U.S. Congress by calling a war something else, for example, "involvement", "conflict", "intervention", "peace-keeping mission", "rescue mission", "advisors sent to assist in humanitarian aid", etc., etc., etc.

My point in the generalization above is simply that drafting citizens tends to more quickly bring wars to an end. Knowing your son, parents, other relatives, friends, acquaintances, hometown citizens, neighbors and so on who are taken into a war they may or may not agree to and with, tends to create a nation-wide and necessary conversation that goes something like this: "What are we doing over there in …. Afghanistan, Iraq, Pakistan, Somalia, Korea, Vietnam….? "Why are we there? What's the objective? Is it worth it? Does…..threaten our security? Is this the humane tack to take? Do we cause more destruction and loss of life than can ever justify the intervention in the first place? Can we afford the loss of life of our soldiers in this effort? Is this really a war for: oil, hurt pride, imperialism (harsh word and not politically correct), macho bluster, political expedience or…. What else?"

So, does that make me an isolationist wanting to roll up our country into a defensive shell? Not by a long shot. Efforts for peace are underfunded. Efforts to provide humanitarian aid are underfunded. Efforts to create conditions for democracy to emerge are underfunded. Despite President Eisenhower's warning, the military – industrial complex is overfunded. The Defense Department is overfunded and over-controlled by defense contractors.

So, these are stories largely representing my attempt to cast a critical and perhaps humorous light on the military, and my experience while caught up in the military machine.

Hundreds of other books about our military, describing bravery, heroism, and honor have been published. This work is not meant to diminish, in any fashion, the noble sacrifice of our men and women in the military, past or present.

But, take a look at what kind of things went on. Hope you enjoy.

Vietnam Calling: It's The National Guard for Me

By: John James

For: Lynne and the "kids"

Table of Contents

Chapter 1: Uncle Sam Wants You (Me?)

The year was 1967. I was in graduate school. I was getting drafted. I was scared. What could I do? Vietnam was a Southeast Asia holocaust. The U.S. was fighting a losing war. Losing hundreds, then thousands of soldiers. Decimating an innocent population of civilians. Fighting North Vietnamese, Viet Cong and South Vietnamese supporters of the North. Fighting political corruption, despots, war profiteers, and others. At home, America was divided. Some wanted the war to escalate "Bomb them back into the stone age! Nuke em! Nuke all of em!" Some in America wanted us to get out. "Just declare victory and come home! Make love, not war! Bring our soldiers home! Peace now!" Demonstrations were spreading across the land.

Most Americans followed the war in the news, on the radio – daily casualty reports, and more importantly, on television. Reports of bombings, military maneuvers, sad stories of caskets coming home, although the military quit allowing news coverage of the returning war dead arriving in Dover, Maryland.

Lots of Americans went numb. Tried to not pay attention to "the war to stop Communism. The war to prevent the dominoes of other countries falling to communism if South Vietnam were to be lost."

The propaganda was fierce – all around. From the political right, the liberal left, even the "silent majority" became less silent, and on and on.

I didn't want to be drafted. I didn't want to go to Vietnam. I wanted to finish graduate school studying Psychology. I wanted to teach at a college, do some research, primarily with how we can improve learning skills in children, and do some private therapy/counseling.

My draft board thought I needed to be a soldier. Somehow they just knew my contribution would be ever-so- valuable. "You could make a difference young man! This is for your country, after all! You'll look good in a uniform! Your parents will be so proud of you!"

I wasn't convinced. Not even close. I just wanted to finish my education and training. I was even willing to join after grad school and my post-doc training. "No, son, your country needs you now." It looks to me like the war is going to be around for a few (or more) years. "You're not listening young man. You are 1A. That means you're next. Get ready! Start packing."

My Psychology Department Chairperson wrote a strong letter asking for a delay from my draft board. No response.

I'm getting drafted! What do I do? Other graduate students told me "Get in the National Guard and take your chances." What? "Find a Texas National Guard unit, join voluntarily, and hope your unit isn't called up to active duty and sent to Vietnam." Good idea, even though I don't want to be in the military. The military is fine if that's what you want to do – it's good for some people – just not for me. I want to … Oh, I already said that – can't I just follow my dream, not Presidents Kennedy, Johnson, and Nixon's? No, I guess not.

I'm getting drafted. They're getting closer. Do I run away to Canada like many others are doing? No, I can't do that. I want to be a psychologist – not a fugitive. Besides, I like my country. My country does most things right – just not this useless, horrific war. Canada is out. I'm not doing that. What I will do is try to find a National Guard unit, hopefully near school. What a shock. Everybody else is trying the same thing it seems. I call this unit, that unit, that other unit 100 miles away from my school! What responses do I get? "You're wasting my time Junior – the waiting list has over 400 names on it. Even if the war goes on, forget it – you're going to Vietnam. Have a good time. You like hot weather?"

Right, if I have to travel over 100 miles each weekend they meet, so be it. NO luck – no openings – forget it!

That's when my friend Jim, also a grad student, asked me over a cup of coffee down in the bowels of the library, studying for an upcoming exam.. "Are you desperate?" I said "are you crazy? Of course I'm desperate! I will be getting my draft notice any day now!" I hope they lose my letter that opens with "Greetings… "Yes, I'm desperate." Jim took another swallow of his long-cold coffee and said "How about the Airborne?" "Airborne what?" I responded. "Sounds like a virus. What are you talking about Jim?" Trying to act altogether too cool, he said Texas has a few units they call the Texas Army Air National Guard. It's Army Reserve but they jump out of airplanes – they're Airborne."

I was in shock. I was dumbstruck, my head filled with peanut butter. I couldn't think. Really. All I could do was look at him. For how long, I don't know. Some period of time later, he stood, and asked "more coffee?"

Eventually, all I could say was "could we talk about this after the test?" "Sure" So, we did. He told me what he knew about the Air National Guard, and I decided to look into it. About 30 miles from the University was a small, rural Texas town. And, sure enough, it contained a National Guard Armory and a unit of the Texas Army Air National Guard. I called ahead, made an appointment with the recruiting sergeant,

Sergeant Adams. The next day, I drove out to see the Sergeant and get all the information I needed. He had two openings, both as a rifleman, so I joined on the spot. It was April's Fool's Day! I'm in the Army now. I can't believe it. I'm actually in the military with MOS (Military Occupational Status) as a rifleman parachutist – after all the training – 6 months of active duty. But then, I can return to graduate school, finish my training to be a psychologist, but I have to be in the military for 6 years, subject to call-up for active duty at any time during the 6 years, and subject to activation for years after I fulfill my 6 year obligation. But I also have to jump out of airplanes – be a paratrooper! I was a desperate man. I received my temporary 6 month leave from graduate school and began the wait for "orders to be cut," meaning I would be off to …what I wasn't sure.

The letter came.

I finished up what I could for my classes, fellowship job, said a very difficult good-by to my wife, and got on a bus to go to Dallas for more "processing." As I was to find out, I was indeed to come to feel "processed" – like maybe Velveeta.

My wife left the day before to stay with my parents in San Diego, Ca during my active duty time. I was packing my things literally hours before I was to "report to the bus?" when I cut my hand on, of all things, a light switch with a bent metal corner on the switch-plate. I couldn't stop the bleeding, even wrapped in a towel. So I called a fellow grad student to take me to the hospital for stitches. This is ridiculous, I thought. Do I try to get out of going to the Army? How many times do you think that happens? I tried to call the Army Welcome Center from the hospital ER. No answer. So, at the hospital they sew up my hand, 16 beautiful stitches, and my friend takes me back to my apartment. I finish packing what little I was taking with me, and got a ride from the same friend to the bus station.

There are many descriptions of Army life, but one of the most accurate is "Hurry up and wait." The hurrying and waiting was about to begin for real.

I have one worn-out suitcase in my left hand, a bandaged right hand I have to hold at least level with my heart, but the throbbing pain is unrelenting. The hospital had offered a prescription for something much stronger than Tylenol, but I had turned them down, thinking the Army may not like the idea of showing up for duty with a pocket full of strong pain-killers. Big mistake. One of many to come.

Now I'm waiting in the Greyhound Bus Station for my luxury coach to Dallas Army Welcome Station. It's late of course. When it does arrive, I wonder how it made it to the bus station. Dirty, dinged up, belching diesel fumes it limps into the station. The engine finally shuts off (why do buses insist on idling for what seems like hours? Maybe they won't start again?). The driver emerges from the bus, coughs, spits, farts and says "OK let's go folks, we're late. It's now 8:30 pm, and my three fellow passengers and I board the trash strewn antique Conestoga wagon as the driver literally throws our luggage into the side storage compartments. Off we go to Dallas, with me resting my right hand on the empty seat in front of me. I think again, this Tylenol is just not going to do it. Plus, it was now all gone. Great!

We had lots of stops on the 3 hour trip to "Big D," picked up a few more straggling passengers and arrived at the Dallas bus station at 1:45 am. The bus is met by a sleepy looking Army corporal, and the yelling begins.

"How many Army dirt-bags do we have here?" he yells across the bus station waiting room. Four others raise their hands, two of them saying "over here". I'm just watching as this little Corporal Napoleon finds his last soldier, me.

"Alright you numb-nuts, here is your voucher for the Savoy hotel just down the street. Grab your gear and head on down there for the night. Be out front of the hotel at 6 a.m. for your next bus ride. Don't be late. Don't make me have to go to your room to get you. That won't make me happy, and you don't want to do that. Now get lost!"

One of the "soldiers" had the audacity to say to Corporal Napoleon "What? It's 2:00 in the stupid morning. You want us to walk down to a hotel, sleep a couple hours, get up and ready to go at 6 a.m.? You got to be kidding!" The Corporal yelled at him all the way down the street to the hotel.

To use the word hotel is a misnomer. The room was like a closet, two twin beds per room, two soldiers per room. I didn't sleep. My hand was aching so I just sat – on the floor. The room had no chairs. At 5:30 I woke up my roommate, Todd, and said to him "you may want to get up, it's 5:30." Friendly Todd said " Go away!" I did. I got on the bus at 6:00. The corporal was still screaming at my roommate Todd through the lobby, onto the bus and for another 15 minutes on the bus. Todd was without a shirt, shoes, socks, and was still getting sort of dressed as we drove away from the front of the hotel – headed to the Dallas Reception Station.

Reception Station
Dallas, Texas

It was April, 1969.

I just love the names the Army can give to many of its operations, equipment, personnel, and so on. A good example was our first stop off the bus in Dallas- the Reception Station. I'm here to be evaluated for fitness for duty in the U.S. Army. If I pass I'll leave in a few days for…what? It has such a welcoming feel that belies the reality. I didn't feel welcome, or wanted, or much of anything positive. Of course, to expect otherwise would become abundantly clear with further contact (literal and figural). We were assigned a service number, and our names seemed to disappear.

The physical exam was a joke. But the joke was on us – the fodder for that Southeastern War debacle.

We were processed, and then processed again. Like a Waring blender, we were received and blended. We filled out forms, took "tests", waited in lines to take hearing tests, vision tests, and even flat feet exams.

In the vision test, we were asked to read letters on the familiar Snellen Chart hung on the wall. The recruit in front of me in line was having trouble reading the letters. The examining corporal yelled "move closer to the wall." He kept moving closer until his nose was about 12" from the wall before he could get the letters right. The Corporal stamped "PASS" on his form and then shouted to me "Next." He saw I was holding a pair of reading glasses in my hand and he said "let me see those." He looked through them, grabbed my paperwork and wrote "Reading glasses two week." I pointed to the two words misspelled and foolishly said "you have two typos there Corporal." Very big mistake. It was maybe 5-6 minutes he yelled at me. I passed the vision test – easily.

Next was the auditory exam. In a group of about 30 men, a sergeant told us "Listen up ladies, this here is the hearing test. If you got two ears you're going to pass. When it's your turn, you're going in this little booth. If you hear a beep in your right ear, push the right button. If you hear a beep in your left ear, push the left button. Do any of you idiots not know your right ear from your left ear?" I almost laughed out loud – a close call. Incredibly, somebody raised his hand. The sergeant went to this poor guy and slapped his right ear and said "this is your right ear dummy," slapped his left ear and said "this is your left ear you moron!"

Sergeant Auditory Expert strutted back to the front of our group and announced "This is how this is going to work. You're going in my little room here, and you're not leaving until you pass! Got it?"

We all passed, but just for fun I never pressed the left button for tones in the left ear. Was I surprised he stamped "PASS" on my form? Not hardly.

After the Army IQ test was graded by the end of the day, a sergeant pulled me aside and said "I think you should apply to change your MOS from Infantry to Intelligence," No thanks, sergeant", I said. "Good man", he said, "go Infantry all the way – born killers." "Right, sergeant", I said. He smiled - the first one I had seen all day.

Next, after a few more days at the Savoy, back on the bus for a guided trip to Ft. Polk, Louisiana.

Welcome to the U.S. Army

Going to Louisiana by bus? That's right! A bus, almost full, loaded with young soldiers to be, headed for Basic Training at the most infamous training base for recruits bound for Vietnam -Ft. Polk, near the woods and swamps of Louisiana, located a few miles from Leesville, also known as "Diseaseville."

Long bus ride, through the huge state of Texas, getting greener as we travel east. Also, warmer – much warmer, and more humid. Nice weather to travel to the south – the summer. The bus was air conditioned, but didn't work. Only a few windows would slide down so there was little breeze, and what there was, was in the extremely warm range.

Many hours later, we arrived at Ft. Polk. Primitive barracks and buildings carved out of a forest of trees and swamps.

We arrived at around 4:00 a.m. to the sound of more yelling. "Get off the bus, get off the bus you maggots. Move! Move! Move your asses now!"

Two Drill Sergeants (Training Sergeants) yelled us into an empty classroom and told us "Welcome to Ft. Polk. Your mommies aren't here – no more Mommy's babies here, you scum. This is your first classroom. Sleep if you can, tough shit if you can't. We'll be back at 5:00 a.m. to say hi again. Good night you little snots." With that they left, locked the door (Why? Where would we go?), and we sat in school chairs and desks, and thought our own thoughts. Like, "What am I doing here?"

I'll summarize 8 weeks of Basic Training. PT (Physical Training), marching, running, camping in the woods, classes in how to salute, shoot a rifle, shoot a machine gun, shoot a grenade launcher, throw hand grenades, map reading and navigation, how to use gas masks, how to clean weapons, and how to survive in the jungle. I'll describe this later, but, basically I was a terrible soldier. My goal was simple – get through it, go back home to my wife, and get back in school.

Chapter 2: Basic Training

Basic Training consisted of the first step in the process of learning to become a soldier in the U.S. Army. I was assigned to undergo 8 weeks of Basic Infantry training at Ft. Polk, Louisiana. I tried to view this as a vacation in the country. Here are some of my holiday highlights.

You Don't Want This Bunk, Whitey

All of us new recruits assembled in a huge group outside the overnight classroom. We are yelled into smaller groups and assigned to Drill Sergeants and then to barracks. This is all done very carefully, for example "You 30 dipshits get in that barracks and find a bunk. Go!"

I take my meager possessions into the barracks, see most of the bunks on the first floor are already taken and head up to the second floor of the two-story barracks. I throw my stuff on the first available bunk. One African-American on my left, one African-American on my right, one African-American on the bunk above me. That's OK with me, but another "Brother" strolls over to me, grins and says "You don't want this bunk, Whitey. This floor is for the Brothers. You're not! Bye Bye."

I left, back down to the first floor and finally found an empty bunk. I was to quickly learn the U.S. Army was officially integrated, but many of the soldiers and training personnel saw it differently.

Filling Out Forms

From the first day of Basic Training, to the last day of training, most days (well, maybe not most) we were to fill out forms. I often wondered where they stored all those forms. The paperwork was incredible. Often, we were led through the filling out of the forms, line by line, sometimes word by word.

In front of the classroom, Corporal Ditto says "I'm going to pass out forms 1642A. He passes them out one by one. I guess passing out form 1642A cannot be done by rows. From the pile of forms in his hands, they don't look scarce or endangered. Five minutes later, "Alright does everybody have form 1642A? If you don't have form 1642A, raise your hand. Anybody?" There are about 25 of us in the room. How hard can it be to look over 25 seats? The answer? Very hard, I guess. Corporal is finally ready to move on." Now find the front of the page. There are questions on the front side and the back side. Find the front side. The front side has a 1 in the top right hand corner. Find the front side with the 1 on it. OK, everyone got the front side? If you don't have page 1, you're on the wrong page." (Remember, this is one sheet of paper). "Look at the top of the page where it says 'NAME'. Find the box that says FIRST NAME. Got it? Now put your first name in that box where it says FIRST NAME. Don't put a nickname or part of your first name, but your Army name. Like if your first name is 'Robert', don't put 'Bob', or 'Bobby', or 'Robbie' or anything but your real name – like 'Robert'. Minutes later, "Now on page one still, at the top, next to the box that you just filled in with your first name, find the box that says LAST NAME." We proceed.

Really, this happened. So, maybe 3 hours later, Corporal Ditto announces "Now we're moving on to the hard part. The Army needs information about your past STD's - sexually transmitted diseases. I will tell you about STD's, OK? The hours crawl along.

KP Day One

"James, is that your name?" (it was on my uniform but must have been hard to read – it had 5 letters) "Yes, Drill Sergeant. That's a real hard name." Big mistake (but I would eventually learn to just keep my mouth shut almost all the time). Drill Sergeants don't really want you to talk, even when you think they do – maybe also when they think they do). "Sergeant Belcher (really!) says – "Oh, a comedian here. Listen up everybody – our Easy company – (E Company – The Army is big on abbreviations) has a comedian – a real funny guy. James, huh? Forget about being funny, there's nothing funny here – forget funny – forget anything but what I tell you! Are you still funny?" Silence from me. "Can you hear me?" Literally screaming a half inch from my face. Silence from me. "You're learning now shitface," he says. "I'll do the talking – you got that?" says Sergeant Belcher. "Yes," I say. Another big mistake. "Yes! What do you mean 'yes'. My name is 'yes, Drill Sergeant.' Now do you have your head out of your ass? It's yes! Drill Sergeant." "Yes, Drill Sergeant," I say. "What, I can't hear you – What? I scream as loud as I can "Yes! Drill Sergeant." He gives me a little smile and simply says "Oh, f---k you, asshole!" He starts to walk away toward the other recruits, then turns around, looks at me, apparently not through with me yet (far from it). "James, I don't want you in my presence. Report for KP – Now! Go!" I simply held up my bandaged hand. He looked at it, looked and me and said "What is this? Do you have a boo-boo? Poor baby. Are you pretending you can't do KP because of a little boo -boo? Now that's funny James. Take that stupid bandage off! Now, take that fake bandage off!" I do, and he grabs my hand, looking carefully at the stitches and rips a few loose and blood begins weeping. The skin is red and gnarled and puffy. He holds my hand up for everyone else in the barracks to see and shouts "Everyone take a look at this little baby boo- boo. In "the Nam" this is nothing! Nothing I tell you. James, get out of my barracks and report to the mess hall for KP. Go!"

I do report to the kitchen, am yelled at some more by the Mess Sergeant and assigned to wash pans, pans and more pans. My cut is bleeding in the huge sink, and another soldier tells the Mess Sergeant. The Sergeant comes over, grabs my hand, looks at that blood in the water and yells to me "Get your ass out of my f-----g mess hall!"

I go back to the barracks, report in to Sergeant Belcher and the yelling begins again.

Hurry Up and Wait

Anyone who has served in the military knows what the phrase "hurry up and wait" means. It could be the official mantra or logo of the Army. It could be sewn on the fatigues of every soldier. Literally, it was accurate to say our major set of responsibilities was to hurry up all the time, regardless of what we were doing, only to be followed by the height of boredom - - doing absolutely nothing. Waiting for the next "hurry up" activity was most of our job.

A good example was "chow". Always, always, always we were to "hurry up and eat." "Eat faster you useless slugs". I would occasionally see a half-eaten meal taken from a soldier who was "eating too slowly."

If you were hungry, you learned to eat fast – real fast – or not at all.

Running

This is a difficult one. Not really. We ran with every possible combination of equipment. Sometimes a little, sometimes a lot. Hint: Not in fancy running shoes – but combat boots! We even had a couple of classes in how to treat blisters - our constant companions. Sometimes at night in the barracks, some would compare the size of their blisters. I didn't need that. I took a pass.

For the first 4 weeks we had to run everywhere we went. To training sites, to chow, to pick up our mail. If you took a step walking, someone would be screaming in your ear. Also, the longer the line you had to run to, the faster you were expected to run. I loved the discipline training.

March On 1

The Army taught us many helpful life skills. Two of them were how to march and how to salute. I have used these skills so often since my time in green fatigues. I am so grateful.

Learning to salute took two and a half days, interspersed with lots of running and other P.T. At first thought, an uninformed person would think it should only take, maybe an hour, to learn this complex skill. Not true. The hand and the fingers need to be so straight – and together. And fingers all together need to barely touch the special spot on the right side of the forehead. Not too high or too low. And not in your eye – for sure. I finally got it right, with no injuries to eye, fingers, or forehead.

Now, marching was a different story. How many times did I hear something like "No!, your other left!" Left- right –left-right, march here and there, and everywhere. It was the turns that I found to be a challenge. Left turn, right turn, half-turn, and face on. It seemed I never could end on the right step. Eventually, I got it, but maybe it was so hard because I have no concept of rhythm. I couldn't possibly remember how many hours we marched, but it always seemed to be forever. Sore feet were with us daily. So we had classes on how to care for our feet. Finally, something useful.

Oh well, all to teach discipline. That we needed, when I consider the rag-tag bunch that started out.

March On 2

It's really true. If you're in the Army, you do a tremendous amount of marching. Just in Basic alone I would love to know how many miles we marched. A ten mile march in a day came to be considered an "easy day." Twenty miles in a day was considered more of a challenge, especially when "90/90". That's at least 90 degrees and 90 plus humidity. We called these "forced marches" because it seemed they had to "force us to do it." The Army used the term "hurried march."

Regardless, I would go into an "automatic pilot" mode to not focus on all the unpleasantness. A huge benefit of doing this was to be able to tune out all the grumbling and griping going on, constantly, around me. The first few weeks I was interested in how creative the complaining could be. After that, it was tiresome.

It should be said, complaining and being in the Army are simpatico bedfellows. A friend once asked me "Why don't you complain like the rest of us?" I responded, "If I come up with a new one, you'll hear it."

One last observation about marching. The very short soldiers had to work a lot harder than those of us over 6 ft tall in both the length of the stride the Army required, and, therefore, the number of steps taken on long treks.

I will admit that all those walking (and running) miles did create a level of fitness I had never before achieved. I was losing more weight, but the muscle mass remained well-hidden.

Salt

The heat really was oppressive – and as it clearly became evident, dangerous. The middle of summer at Ft. Polk, temperatures at or around 100 degrees, humidity 80 % + day after day. It seemed some of us could sort of get used to the heat. Not me. Each day was a challenge. We had to take salt tablets each day, every day. Two horse pills of salt three times per day. Then, during training we would sweat it out. Our fatigues, in all the right places, would turn white with the salt perspiration, and get stiff as it dried.

The long marches were always interesting because wherever we went, Jeep medic ambulances with big red crosses on the sides and top would follow us. Sure enough, each march had its share of individuals who would "fall out", and drop to the ground because of the heat. Some with serious cases of heatstroke. The latter were loaded in the medic ambulance and shuffled off to the hospital, and the next ambulance would pull up to the back of our marching formation ready for the next one to fall. Heat stroke was considered by our Training Sergeant as a moral and toughness failure. Just another thing that was difficult to understand. But then, trying to understand much of what we experienced was actually pointless.

Bayonet Practice

This part of Basic Training involved first pretending a broomstick (without a broom at the end) was really a rifle with a bayonet fixed at the barrel end which we used to charge hay figures sort of looking like humans. This training was excellent for those who had watched too many John Wayne war movies. It was important to scream "AAAAHHH!! " as loudly as you could as you stuck your broomstick into the "hay man."

The louder you screamed and the harder you jabbed your broomstick the better your "kill", and therefore, the better soldier you were bound to be.

After two days of this excellent practice they issued broken rifles and bayonets. Look out, a weapon look-alike showed up. We then had a class in bayonet safety. Is that an oxymoron? I know some of the ways a few young men handled the bayonets, the moron part fit.

Now we affixed the bayonets to the end of the broken rifles and attacked those "hay men" again. I tell you, they never stood a chance.

During one break in the training, a combat vet back from Vietnam was talking to a few of us as we were refilling our water canteens. One soldier asked the Vet. "Corporal what do you think of this bayonet training?" He laughed, and in a moment of honesty said "If the VC are that close to you, your ass is grass already. Bayonets are for opening C-Rations – that's it! Now go back and kill some more hay bales!

We went back with renewed vigor and confidence.

Pugil Sticks

Four-foot poles with 6" padded ends were called pugil sticks and were meant to condition and train us in hand-to-hand combat (see the combat vet's comments above). In a 15 ft- ring we would just try to knock the other soldier down, then hit him again. It did rattle your teeth. Fun. Pugil sticks, to my knowledge, were not issued to our soldiers in Vietnam.

Hand-to-Hand Fighting

The trainers in these exercises taught us how to "parry" (block the attack) of the enemy, throw him to the ground and hit him in the face and neck. Some of us got pretty bruised up in this training. We weren't really supposed to smack our opponent, but some "forgot" about that.

Fortunately, no rifles or bayonets were issued for this training. I can't imagine the injuries that would have involved. Several young men were magically transformed into Bruce Lee imitators. It was really quite humorous, at times.

Dirt

I'll say this for the Army – they detested dirt. Well, that needs to be qualified. The Army hated dust/dirt in the barracks (the floor especially), on our equipment (especially our weapons), on and around our bunks, in our footlockers, and anything owned by the U.S. Army – but there was one notable exception. Our bodies. Never was there a complaint about us getting wet, muddy or dirty as a result of the training itself.

In fact, we were supposed to get down and get dirty. We did that quite well.

Buckets

I had seen what I thought was rain, growing up in Southern California. Now I know that wasn't really rain. I thought I had seen rain in travels through the Pacific Northwest. Not really there either.

In the forests and swamps of Louisiana I saw "buckets of rain," or "rain in sheets," "rain such that you can't see two feet in front of your face," or "rain whiteouts." I never imagined it was possible to rain that much or that hard or for so long (or so short a time). I've seen rainstorms in TV shows or in movies, but not like what I saw at Ft. Polk. We were all issued ponchos as part of our Boy Scout gear, but using a poncho in these rainstorms was completely useless. It was just impossible to stay dry. After a couple days of wrestling with a poncho, we just gave up. "Let it rain, let it rain…. All our equipment, rifles, extra clothing, all of it totally soaked. The rain would become rivulets, then creeks, then we just got tired of moving away from it and just sat in the water. Eventually it would stop, and eventually we'd get dry. Dried up in the baking sun in the next hour or by the next day.

One night, in the midst of a terrific rainstorm, I was ordered to come into the captain's tent to "man the radio." While trying to talk the military communication language the rain incredibly increased in ferocity. I heard a roar and then felt a wave of water washing over the tent, radios, two boxes of paperwork, and me. The water washed all of the tent contents including me about twenty yards down a wash.

Somehow, I was responsible for all the washed away or damaged equipment. Our fearless Captain had ordered his tent pitched in a small, but clearly evident dry creek bed.

As the Captain was screaming at me "How could you let this happen?" there were lots of things I wanted to say. What I did say was "my training failed me." Captain Marvel was taken aback, looked hard at me, turned a deeper shade of red and hollered "are you blaming this on the U.S. Army?" I didn't answer. He repeated the question, only louder. In this case, I figured I had to say something – he wasn't just going to go away and leave me alone. So, I said "The U.S. Army provides the best training in the world, I have just not maximized to the fullest, everything I should have learned – so far."

Captain looked at me quizzically. He had part of the answer he was looking for. It was somebody's fault, and it wasn't his. He got in my face and said "you are a major f---kup" "Yes, sir" I said. He walked away.

Now I could go look in the mud for my rifle. It's a real big problem if you lose your rifle.

I've heard stories about the mind just "going numb", or perhaps it is a state of hypnosis, or maybe the mind just shuts down in some adverse situations. That happened to me on long, hot, difficult forced marches, or hours in a relentless rainstorm. I would find myself disconnected from the unpleasantness of the situation, and just feeling a nothingness that seemed to help me cope.

Chow

What can I say? It was not good. No, correct that – it was awful. A favorite in the morning was what was commonly called "shit on a shingle." Some gravy concoction with small pieces of some meat product poured over white bread. We had about 4 minutes to eat – and lots of Training Sergeants yelling at us to eat faster. Things like "get out of my mess hall you fat pigs." I went to the Army sort of skinny, and came back a bean pole. A lot of us developed very baggy pants. Don't bother asking for new clothes. Not allowed, just tighten that belt.

At lunch we often were served "Donkey Dicks." This was some sort of hot dogs on steroids, or sausage or…. something. It was always so interesting that meat products were so often unidentifiable. We gave up asking each other "what is this shit?"

Dinner was often hamburgers and mashed potatoes. On KP duty I saw what potatoes were used to make the mashed potatoes, so I knew to be careful there. But the "hamburger meat" had some kind of oatmeal-like extender added. Some form of "hamburger helper" that tasted sort of like moldy cheerios.

Also, on KP duty (I spent a lot of time there) I saw how they handled what was some sort of beef. Anything dropped on the floor was subject to the 5 second rule – or maybe longer. Pick it up, brush it off – or not – and continue on.

Dining in the field was a 5-star affair. Get out your mess kit, and if we were lucky enough to not have cold C-Rations, go through the line and have something or somethings plopped in your (small aluminum) kit.

It really was true we usually didn't know what it was. "Hot meal" did not mean it was hot or even warm. By the time the mess trucks got to us out in the field, it was not hot and had congealed. One fine rainy day, when I was feeling particularly tired and disgusted, I commented to a mess server (a private like me) "this is congealed." He looked at me, flushed angry red and yelled "What the shit does that mean? Take this!", and he dumped a large spoonful of – something – in my water cup. I had a "lite lunch" that day. That's OK.

If we weren't lucky enough to get a "hot" meal in the field, and had C-Rations (Combat Rations) in green tins we sometimes found dates stamped on the tin bottoms – 1945 or 1946. Scary – especially what was labeled "Potted Beef." I cannot possibly describe what it looked like. I got to where I wouldn't even open a tin labeled "Potted Beef". The canned peaches were often what I could eat in the C-Rations. But how could they be preserved since WWII? I tried not to think about it much.

One more chow story is all I can tolerate. One lunch we were told by the Platoon Sergeant "you lucky bastards get great chow today – real spaghetti, and its good – I tasted it." He wasn't lying. It was spaghetti, it was hot and it was good. After lunch, he said "now we're going to run it off."

We went on a 5-mile run. All along the route there were soldiers stopping to give back their lunch. Army humor.

Guard Duty

Ft. Polk was operating under the interesting belief that the fort and all roads into the facility needed protection. From what form of invasion, attack, or danger was never clear. The reality was the opposite- that some soldiers were trying to get out (A.W.O.L. – Absent Without Official Leave).

So, out in the darkest of dark nights, in groups of two, we put on M.P. helmets, arm bands and unloaded broken rifles to guard a swampy road into one of the most Godforsaken places on earth. I had a perfect record in my role of protecting Ft. Polk. Not a single enemy got past me. At least none I knew about. If anybody showed up, I wondered what I would do. I guess I could throw my helmet at them – or better yet, my rifle with no bullets. I should also mention we had no radios to call for help in case of an invasion. Walk back and forth across a deserted road in the middle of a swampy forest for four hours at a time in the dead of night was just more good training – for what was unclear.

Fire Watch

When we slept in the barracks, each of the two floors was required to have a fire watch guard. This meant, in two hour shifts, the assigned fire guard was responsible for walking the floor, prepared to alert the men in the unlikely event of a fire. I never saw or heard of any building having a fire, but, most nights, some fire watch guard in some barracks would fall asleep, fail to awaken the next guard, and trouble would ensue.

Occasionally, a fire watch guard would try to cut his two-hour shift short and just awaken the next guard early. That usually caused a ruckus, as well. This was just more good training in how to look out for fires, like if I was going to get a job in a National Forest in an isolated fire-watch tower.

Mail Call

Each day in training was a full day of physical exercises, classes, marching, and fun-filled fellowship with other All-American soldiers and patriots. Clearly, the high point of each evening of training, when we weren't out spending the night in the woods and swamps, was mail call. Some soldiers got mail daily, or almost so. I was in that group. Most got no mail regularly, some not at all.

It was sad to see the anticipation in so many faces followed by hurt, disappointment, and even anger. And then there were the young men who received bad news. Not enjoyable to watch.

Much "attitude" was shown around mail-call, with some wanting to read their letters out loud to anyone who would listen. Most who did receive mail, sought quiet as they read and re-read every word. Some smiling, whooping with good news, some were quietly weeping. Sometimes a fight would emerge, broken up by other men, or the Drill Sergeants who had a room at the end of the barracks. So many emotional ups-and-downs during and after mail call.

Haircuts and Sand in My Pockets

Most people have seen on TV or in movies how new soldiers are relieved of their hair in a matter of seconds. True. We are in four lines for four "barbers" and had four Drill Sergeants yelling at us when the next barber was free to "get in the f-----kg chair." The haircuts were free, along with everything else. No extra charge for the nicks and scrapes that went along with the salon experience.

What's more, the experience was repeated weekly for four weeks. After that, we were expected to get our own haircuts. What? Why would I do that? It was cut as close as it could be without being shaved. So, I skipped the haircut in week 5 and 6. Another mistake.

"James, are you some stupid fag from San Francisco? Are you a hippie? Do you think you're a commie hippie in my U.S. Army? Your hair is too long – it's almost over your ears (not even close). Just look at you. You know what I do with commie hippies?" (Silence from me of course). "I make them put sand in their pockets" he says. I'm thinking, but not saying anything out loud, ("where did you come up with that idea you ignorant imbecile?)"

Sergeant must have read my thoughts because next he yells "You probably wonder why I do that, don't you, you pregnant fairy" (What?). "Well, I'll tell you – long hair can weigh you down, and then you can't run as fast when the Viet Cong are chasing your ass in the jungle. So, I'm giving you practice at carrying less weight, so you'll be a quicker asshole, and maybe even come back from the Nam to thank me" (Right – count on that). "But, you probably won't come back you sorry excuse for a soldier. Now get out your Entrenching Tool (small Army shovel we carried around with our other gear), go over to that sand pile and fill all your pockets with sand. All of them – all full, you got that?" That's what I did and then reported back to him. "Now James start running around the barracks. I'll tell you when to stop – Got it!?"

That sand was heavy. Eventually, I fell down, the Sergeant found me and said "James, get a haircut by tomorrow and get that f--king-- sand out of your pockets! You must really be stupid – putting sand in your pockets!"

Driver's License

During a break in the ongoing physical training our sergeant got us in formation one day with "Fall-in maggots," and importantly announced "I'm looking for four volunteers." Now, as an aside, I learned very quickly NEVER VOLUNTEER! FOR ANYTHING! It took some young men a long time, if ever, to learn this. The sergeant droned on, "You volunteers must have a driver's license. You must have a valid driver's license from whatever state you're from. All clear on this? Now, raise your hand if you want to volunteer." I'm thinking to myself "Man, I hope there are some volunteers so I don't get 'volunteered'" which happens when there are no volunteers. Several hands go up. They are pulled aside and the sergeant says "You four report to Corporal Sangay in Maintenance, Building B-2."

They take off running. "Good luck," I'm thinking. "You're going to need it." About 45 minutes later we saw all four volunteers pushing wheelbarrows full of rocks across the marching field, and then back again. All good training.

Where Did All That Money Go?

Payday was always an exciting time. We would line up, of course, and when we got to the front of the line, a 'Paymaster Lieutenant' would be sitting at a beat-up desk and I would stand at attention, salute, and say "Private Stone reporting for pay." The bored officer would not even look at me and say "sign here" and hand me a pay envelope "loaded" with cash. Something under $100 as I recall. Not bad for a month's effort.

Now what would you imagine an Army company of about 120 men , largely uneducated, tired, sleep deprived, unhappy, disillusioned and surly young men do with all that money?

Three things: 1. Buy beer 2. Buy pizza 3. Buy comic books

The PX (Post Exchange -- a glorified convenience store) would be packed to overflowing after payday. The watered-down beer would flow, the pizzas were purchased in two's and three's, and comic books appeared everywhere in the barracks that night. Donald Duck, Little Lulu, Superman were very popular. Lots of trading conducted over the next few days. Lots of bargaining, lots of arguing also. Many of these young men came from impoverished and poor educational environments, and many could not read or only minimally read. I was often asked to help men read some of the "bigger" words in the comic books (and letters from home). Sad. There's a whole different America out there – one I knew little about but was now exposed to.

Sick Call

Each morning, sick call was announced by the platoon sergeant. I say announced because it was not put in the form of a question, like "Is there anyone who needs to go on sick call?" This obviously meant "Does anyone really f--king need to see a medic?" Not to see a Doctor – to see a doctor you would have to be dead and couldn't answer any questions at all.

Early in Basic Training, a few actually asked if they could go on sick call. In 99% of the cases that was a big mistake. In the Army, being sick was not looked on at all favorably. Strongly discouraged? Not really. Punished? Sometimes strongly? Truly.

It soon became very evident that if you didn't really need hospitalization for a very serious illness or injury, stay away from sick call. Just "gut it out" as best you can. I saw so many coming back from sick call with two things: 2 aspirin and a boatload of harassment. "Oh, pretty boy are you sickypoo? Hey you lazy piece of shit, why don't you rest right now on the ground. Go ahead, lie down right here in the dirt. You need to take it easy and get a little sun – you know, some vitamin C. You weak mama's boy, here can you lift this toothbrush? You can? Good – now go clean the bathroom with it. Are you sick little boy? Do you need your blanket and pacifier? How about you just suck your thumb instead? I've run out of pacifiers – I'm so sorry. Just sit there and suck your thumb til I tell you to stop. Maybe that will help you feel better. You just keep sucking that thumb until you feel better, then come and tell me when you're better – OK?"

I think you see how it worked. I once saw a young man break his leg falling from an obstacle course net we were to climb over, and as he was rolling around on the ground, two training sergeants were screaming at him "Get up! Get up!" They only quit yelling at him when this poor guy pulled up his fatigues pants leg and we all saw a bone sticking out of his lower leg. After weeks of recovery, he had to start Basic all over again.

Get In That Long Line

The Army is a big believer in lines. Get in line, wait in that line, but hurry up while you're in line. Formations were just lines. Lines for chow, lines for injections, for inspections, for haircuts, for clothes to be issued, for mail, for pay, for just about everything. I have wondered how many hours I waited in some line or another in Basic. The only good thing about waiting in line was you wouldn't be doing anything worse.

To this day, I will not wait in a long line. If I see a long line at a bank, or grocery store or wherever, I'll come back later. I just won't do it.

Where Are My Shot Records?

The U.S. Army believes in discipline – and injections. I wish I had kept a record of all the shots I got, especially in the first two weeks, because I know the Army didn't keep very good track.

At the time, the Army was using some sort of air gun for shots. We waited, of course, in long lines for our "preliminary shots." I made the mistake of asking the Drill Sergeant while in line "What are these shots for?" Another early mistake. What the hell do you care, you stupid recruit? Just shut up, stay in line and get your f--king shots," yells my health-conscious sergeant.

A few men had a powerful fear of shots. Two near me in line fainted, one just as the air gun injector went "Phttt." Down he went. I saw two men sneak out of the line go to the rear of the line to postpone the inevitable.

I don't know how many different shots were in the "Phttt" of the air gun shot pistol, but all of us had two very sore arms for days. For a few hours it was hard to even lift an arm.

How did the Army deal with sore arms? Pull-ups of course. We all "Double-timed" (ran) over to the obstacle course and did as many pull-ups as we could (Not many).

The next day at roll-call, our friendly Drill Sergeant calls me out of formation to demand (hollering) "Why didn't you get your shots yesterday, James? What'd you do, sneak out of the line and hide somewhere? For this question I really did not have an answer. But wait, I did. "Drill Sergeant, I did get my shots yesterday, look at my arm" pointing to the welts.

"I don't want to see your Twinkie arm. The Army says you didn't get your shots yesterday, so you didn't. Now, report to the Infirmary – NOW! and get your shots!

I get to the infirmary, report in, and am asked "Why didn't you get your shots yesterday like everybody else in your company?" says the PFC (Private First Class) at the Infirmary desk. I explain again. "Well too bad, let me see your arms." I show him. "Too bad soldier, go to Room 1 behind me to get your shots."

The medic looks at my arm and says "hold still I'm going to try to line up my gun here to put them in the same place on your arms." I stare at him. He laughs and said "just kidding, I'll try to miss these places where it's swollen and where you didn't get your shots yesterday." Thank goodness for small favors. Not fun – now both arms felt completely useless again – only worse.

Army record-keeping – not the best.

Take That Apart Again

Do you know how in so many movies, you see soldiers taking their weapons apart to clean and then reassemble them? And then do it in the dark? This soldier says "No way" (could I do it). I am a terrible "handy man," who can't repair/fix things, or put children's Christmas toys together, or do even basic mechanical/car maintenance. "If it's not broken too badly, don't try to fix it – just ask my wife to take a look at it" is one of my life lessons. If I see "some assembly required" I run. So, taking a rifle apart was difficult, putting it back together was very difficult; putting it back together in the dark was impossible. So many pieces.

I remember an outside swing/slide set I ordered for our kids one Christmas. When I "finished", it was hardly recognizable. My neighbor disassembled and re-assembled it.

So, I had a few discussions with our Training Sergeants about the proper care of U.S. Army weapons – like the M-16. I recall the first class in cleaning our rifles. "Heads up everyone, today you will learn to clean your best friend – your M-16 combat rifle. They have been manufactured to be very easy to clean, even a moron can do it." I was called that more than once trying to put that rifle back together. I still had pieces left when the sergeant announced "Now we will take it apart again, and put it together again." I didn't have too much to take apart at that point.

I was once asked to help clean an M-60 machine gun. I wouldn't call that a "teachable moment" for me.

Let Me in That Church

During Basic Training, most Sundays were just like any other training day – but on a few Sundays religious services were provided. If they were available, I went. Always! The reasons were simple. It couldn't hurt me – and, attendance at a religious service was the one place that was safe. Safe from being volunteered for any of an infinite number of tasks that are part of Basic. That is, you might think you have a little time off, but the sergeant would come in the barracks and say I need 8 men or 6 men or 12 men – you, you, you…come with me. And off you go to pick up cigarette butts, clean a road sign, paint rocks – or whatever.

So, I would go to any church service, regardless of faith, denomination or whatever represented. The different faiths all shared the same chapel building. I would go to the first service, say it was Catholic, sit through the mass and stay there for the next, say Protestant service. The clergy came to know me pretty well. Once, when asked by a rabbi if I was going to stay for his service too, I said "I sure am, I need it." He smiled and said "I think I get what you mean."

You! Smart Ass – Write my Reports

It was not a good idea for anyone in the U.S. Army to find out you went to college. If a Training sergeant or officer found out, it surely meant extra doses of harassment. "Hey! F---king college boy. If you're so smart what are you doing in the U.S. Army?" (Actually, a good question). "Did you bring your books with you? You're going to read to the gooks in the Nam? You tell those slant-eyes in Vietnam you went to college and they, for sure, won't blow your shit away. They just kill dummies! Can you read this training manual better than me? I bet college kicked you out, and that's why they sent you to me, right? You just forget everything you learned in college. That will only get you killed where you're going. Only peaceniks go to college. I went to college too – the college of how to survive when the Viet Cong want to stick a bayonet up your ass." On and on. The insults, sometimes, were quite humorous. But, don't laugh, whatever you hear.

One of my favorite Training Sergeants somehow found out I was in college when in the process of being drafted. How, I never found out.

"Hey, James get over here. Since you are such a smart ass, you're going to help the Captain write his reports. I said, "Sergeant, I don't know how to write military reports, I'll probably…" "Shut up numbnuts." After training today report to the Captain's orderly at headquarters and don't f-ck up."

I thought to myself "this could work out OK, maybe I'll miss some of the ridiculous training. Why would I think this? I guess because I wasn't fully trained yet.

Anyway, I reported to the Headquarters Quonset hut after training ended about 8:00 p.m. that night. The orderly to the captain, Corporal Toady, hands me a draft of a report by our Captain Marvel and simply says "make this a smart report." "What?" I ask. "Just do it asshole," he says. I got too much to do, so you're going to help out with this paperwork shit."

He hands me a truly incredible document. Immediately, it is clear our Captain was functionally illiterate. "Now what am I going to do with this?" I ask myself. This has trouble for me written all over it, so I decide I'll, at least have some fun with it. I take his jibberish and rewrite it using lots of big words, but it says nothing sensible. I translate his rambling into impressive sounding nonsense. When I finish I take it to the orderly.

He tries to read it and says "this is f--king great. Good job James." Over the next 2 days I wrote 3 more, before it hit the proverbial fan. I was summoned to the Captain and thoroughly "reamed out." My defense was simply "I did the best I could, Sir." He finally gave up and said "get out of my sight you useless prick!" I guess I got fired. Two more days of KP. To me, it was worth it.

Ventriloquism

It would probably be very surprising to many individuals who never experienced the joys of military service, to know that so many hundreds of thousands, perhaps even millions of young people learned ventriloquism in the service.

That's right. This specific skill involves talking, usually complaining to your neighbor in formation, during a march or in a class, without moving your lips.

What a terrific skill to learn and be able to steadily develop over my six years in the service.

Desertion

Contrary to what I heard was "popular opinion," I saw very few desertions. In my Basic training company of about 120, only 1 trainee ran away from the post. He showed up 3 days later, and he argued it wasn't really desertion. He claimed to have hitchhiked into town (Leesville) and went on a three day "bender."

A few of us saw him stumble into the barracks late one night, but the platoon sergeant took him away. I never saw him again. I wonder if he visited Ft. Leavenworth, Kansas. Did he miss the war? Probably not.

Music

There were an almost infinite number of opportunities and topics for conflict among us trainees. The one area about which there were the greatest number of disagreements of varying levels of intensity and/or violence was – music.

Some of the soldiers had radios/boom-boxes and all wanted to play their music when we had time off in the barracks, usually at night. Every popular music form of the day was represented, and therefore created a breeding ground for conflict. Unfortunately, music preferences often followed racial lines and contributed in some measure to racial conflict.

Verbal confrontations grew in volume followed by some pushing and shoving, and occasionally the fists would fly. I remember seeing an occasional radio flying across the barracks, smashing against a wall and breaking to pieces. That was almost always followed by violence. Fortunately, these occurrences were rare – but did occur.

Our barracks sergeant had an interesting solution to one such incident. He collected all the radios in sight and threw them in the trash. It was pretty quiet in the barracks after that – for a while. Until the next payday.

Pet Armadillo

The forests and swamps of Louisiana around Ft. Polk are full of what seemed to be critters of every description. One of the most unusual is the armadillo. This is clearly a prehistoric looking animal which is really a New World placental mammal with an armor shell that looks like leather. The word armadillo is Spanish for "little armored one" and is related to anteaters and sloths. They are wild animals and sometimes we would see them while out on maneuvers and training.

About half-way through the weeks of Basic a friend told me he had spotted a small armadillo out the barracks window while on Fire Watch in the middle of the night. He said the little fellow ran under our barracks building. All the barracks buildings were built up off the ground, about 3 feet or so because of the certainty of attracting any number of animal homesteaders, including the feared coral snakes. The next evening, we again had a report of the armadillo (probably the same one) running under the barracks. When the resident Training Sergeant heard about this miscreant, he got the whole platoon to crawl around under the barracks to look for him.

We found nothing, but the night sightings continued. A local trainee took it on himself to try to meet our visitor. He would put out bits of food in the night, and try to stay awake looking for our armored friend. Eventually, he was able to figure out when our guest would arrive and claimed his goal was to tame him. Sort of like trying to train a mascot. It's not as if we didn't have enough to do, as we were always sleep-deprived. But Louis was persistent in feeding what came to be known as "Louie Louie" named after the oldies song by the same title, sung by The Kingsmen, a garage band of the 60's.

The "Louie Louie" nickname soon became "LL" and Louis claimed his new animal training was going well and after 3 weeks of effort, had "LL" literally eating out of his hand.

That is, until the accident. As we all know, accidents happen. Perhaps especially so when wild animals are involved. About 3:00 a.m. the whole barracks was awakened to the loudest screeching of "he bit me… he bit my finger… oh my hand, he bit my finger off." And, indeed LL had lost half his right-hand index finger. So much for the taming of an armadillo.

Grease Trap

It's true. I wasn't the world's best soldier. Not even close. I've told some stories as examples of that, but I hesitate to tell this one. Why? Because it's embarrassing, and certainly doesn't suggest anything positive about me.

Oh well. Here goes. My footlocker which we all had to maintain was at the foot of our bunks, and mine was judged quite harshly during one surprise inspection, to be "messy and not up to Army standards." I could talk a while about "Army standards," but another time. I must also note, the Army loves "surprise inspections." It must take a lot of planning for all the surprises we encountered, and inspections were just one category.

Anyway, my footlocker was not up to code, and I was assigned KP Duty – again. This time, it wasn't just washing pots and pans, or cleaning floors, or peeling potatoes (yes, I did peel hundreds of potatoes during some of my KP time).

My task this day was entirely new. "James, get out behind the mess hall – you're going to clean the grease trap." " What?" I thought but did not say " is the grease trap?" Patience, James, he will tell you all about it. Maybe even have a class in how to do it properly. No such luck. Two huge cellar-like doors were opened revealing a huge iron pit in the ground. It was about the size of two huge dumpsters side by side. "Your job today, James, is to climb in there and shovel out the trapped grease (the cooks constantly dumped in there), then use this high pressure hose to clean out the whole trap. It's plugged up somewhere in there," said the Mess Sergeant.

As I peered into the pit, about 8 feet deep with at least 2 feet of grease at the bottom, I thought "this is more good training." Not funny. I must have had a quizzical look on my face, because my dear sergeant said "If you're looking for a ladder to get down there, forget it! Just jump in. I'll come back later with the pressure hose. For now, shovel the grease into these buckets," as he pointed to a huge mound of 5-gallon buckets surrounding most of the pit.

I really was puzzled now, and asked "and how do I get the buckets out of the pit?" "That's a need to know question" he said and you just get to work. "What?" "Throw some buckets in, and here's a shovel, now get to work!"

This had to be one of the dirtiest jobs I've ever had – even for the Army. I threw the buckets in, then the shovel. The sergeant, glaring at me yelled "You break that shovel, you pay for it!" I thought to myself, "You can count on that!" "Well" says the friendly sergeant "Jump in soldier!" I did, and splashed grease all the way to my fatigue hat, then slipped and fell on my rear end. I can still, at times, hear him laughing as he went back to the mess hall through the back door. I was just about as angry as I had ever been in my life. I had many thoughts, none of them charitable.

So, I picked myself up, squeezed some of the grease off of me, and took stock of my predicament. I filled buckets for about two hours. I was just a slimy mess of grease. I was getting tired and had to go to the bathroom (the "head"). The sergeant reappeared, peeked into the pit and yelled "you sure are slow!" I couldn't help myself and said "I am, and I'm slippery too and need to use the head." All he did was smile and said "shut up and get back to work." I worked for about another hour, then couldn't really hold it any longer and did what I would come to truly regret. I yelled to the mess sergeant that I was going to take a leak in his grease trap." The sergeant returned "midstream." He started screaming at about the level of a jet engine "you're pissing in my grease trap! You're pissing in my grease trap!

I didn't look at him, zipped up and went back to filling buckets. He kept yelling. And then yelling some more. It went on for far too long, but I refused to look at him. Incredibly, he filed a report with my training Sergeant about me "shitting in his grease trap." Later, the next day, when "interrogated by our company 2nd Lieutenant, I was told, "James, I have a report here that while you were on KP Duty you shit in the grease trap. What do you have to say, private?" I only said "Not true, sir"
"Not true he hollered, what's not true?" "Sir, I did not shit in the grease trap. I urinated in the grease trap." The lieutenant just looked at me, and shook his head. Finally, he said "James, get out of here" So, I did.

I was asked what happened to me by many of my fellow barracks mates. And also, to tell the story – over and over again. (I was becoming a very local celebrity), I was asked what happened after the mess sergeant finished yelling at me, I said "Oh, I was relieved of duty in the grease trap." I thought that was sort of witty.

Leave Me Alone

I heard this many, many times in Basic. Not soldiers talking to Training Sergeants, but soldiers talking (usually yelling) at other soldiers.

It could go something like this:

"Hey, fairy, did you get any mail?" Response: "Leave me alone."

"Hey, Bozo, could you loan me a couple bucks?" Response: "Leave me alone."

"Jones, why are you such a f…kup?" Response: "Leave me alone."

"What's your problem, Williams?" Response: "Leave me alone."

"Roberts, get off your ass and help us clean this floor." Response: "Leave me alone."

"Simpson, are you going on sick call again? You know we all get in trouble when you go." Response: "Leave me alone."

"Jackson, what the f… are you doing? You snore all night you dummy." Response: "Leave me alone."

For a few men/boys, that response could be an early sign of emotional withdrawal and depression.

Young Riley, an 18 year old who looked all of 14, kept saying "Leave me alone" over and over to the point he refused to get out of his bunk. Even with the Training Sergeants yelling at him, punching him and finally dragging him from his bunk. There he lay on the floor, curled up in a fetal position. The MP's finally carried him away.

Rumor had it he died in the hospital. How? Why?

Military Fat Camps?

There were many men in Basic that were "pudgy", some of whom were just clearly obese. The Army's treatment of these men ranged from kidding and teasing, to outright cruelty. Sadly, I saw more than a few cases of the latter.

The present-day U.S. military reports that about 25% of volunteers are rejected because of obesity. Currently we hear national reports of an "obesity epidemic", including children. Some reports say two thirds of all U.S. adults are overweight, and half of those obese.

When I served, the treatment of the obese was simple: Run, exercise the weight off or make life so miserable the men would give up, quit, refuse orders, and be turned over to the Army discipline/court martial system. I wish I knew what happened to these men. I only heard rumors of consequences like being put in military jails or prison system and dishonorably discharged. A few were discharged for "medical" reasons, but only after weeks/months of detention and punishment. The Army's position seemed to be that these individuals were shirking their duty to their country, malingering, trying to avoid Vietnam, were cowards, or had some form of character defect.

One small example follows. A mildly obese 18 year old boy/man from Tennessee who was drafted just couldn't handle the physical demands, in particular, the running. He was usually the last person in our company on any run, and a particularly nasty Training Sergeant would run alongside poor Alex screaming in his ear with every abusive word in his vocabulary. It was heart-breaking to hear. I would push myself to near the front of the pack of runners just to avoid hearing it. And, I was hardly any good at running myself so that took some effort.

Regularly, Alex would "drop out", and simply quit running, often falling to the ground. And, of course, the abuse would increase exponentially. Many times, Alex was just left behind. A few times the medic ambulance that always followed along on our runs would pick him up and take him to the aid station.

Later that night in the barracks we would find him doing the dirtiest clean-up jobs imaginable. Occasionally, Alex was also taken out in the night to run some more. Sad.

During one such punishment run, Alex "lost it" and punched a training sergeant in the mouth. I never saw Alex again. Of course the training staff never talked about the incident. I wonder what happened to him?

As I think about Alex, I wonder what today's military is to do about this obesity problem? What if the all-volunteer military cannot get enough recruits? Are we headed back to a draft? Will the military have to begin training with "pre-training" setting up conditioning programs for the overweight even before they begin their standard training? I have no answers. I wonder if the armed forces are working on this.

I know this is a health issue (e.g. Type II diabetes). Will it become a national security issue?

Chapter 3: AIT (Advanced Infantry Training)

The U.S. Army, as a result of many years of research and development in how to prepare soldiers for war, assembled the model of secondary training after Basic. Soldiers were sent to various types of "advanced" schools ranging from artillery, tanks, aviation, clerical, etc. The greatest number went to AIT, which, of course, was the infantry, or as we were called, "grunts." We eventually came to call ourselves "grunts," "cannon fodder," the "expendables," and so on.

Current warfare is becoming more technical or "surgical" (I love this term), including the use of drones, missiles, and, of course, the ultimate game-changer, nuclear weapons.

So, I was sent to my second school for nine weeks of "advanced" training in how to be a "good soldier grunt." As compared to Basic Training, we heard, every day, about how we were going to train for Vietnam. That is, in fact, where the overwhelming majority of us were going.

Here are some examples of any experiences I had in AIT.

AIT: Yep!

AIT was coming up in a week. All of us were hoping "Graduation Day" from Basic would lead to being relocated to a different Army base – any other base – anything but Ft. Polk. We were all ready to go somewhere, anywhere else.

We gather in the barracks, bottom floor, our Training Sergeant announces "Alright ladies, I have your orders here for the next phase of your training. Let's get this done. Atkinson, Troy – Ft. Polk, lucky you. Aztoris, Michael – Ft. Polk. Well look at that – lots of you get to stay here. Next is… on and on…"Incredibly 116 out of 119, including me assigned to stay here at beautiful Ft. Polk, Louisiana.

I'm stuck. Most of us are stuck in the training grounds for Vietnam. It hits once again, just a little closer. This was not a happy meeting.

Later that same day, we all packed up, and moved about 200 yards to our new barracks, and new/old home for another nine weeks. God help us all.

Leesville

The small town of Leesville was the closest civilization to Ft. Polk. It is probably not a fair assessment, but what little I saw of the town was not positive.

In AIT we finally got a Saturday off and could leave the fort. Two friends and I decided to go into town to see what's there. While waiting at the bus stop (no one had cars during training) to go into town, a car stopped at the bus stop and the driver said "you boys want a ride into town?" "Sure" we all three said. "Hop in" the other male in the passenger front seat said. We all climbed in the back of a souped-up muscle car, a Dodge Charger as I recall.

We roared off down the street toward Leesville. The driver was about 23, with long hair, pock-marked skin on his face, and a wild look in his eyes. I figured he'd been taking something as it became evident he was clearly "wired," talking fast and a bit incoherently. He was talking about a big race coming up and he was going to "kick some ass." His buddy in the front was in worse shape. Maybe a couple years younger than the driver, I now noticed his eyes were fluttering, and he suddenly rolled down his window and started yelling at people in other cars.

All three of us in the back seat were getting very uncomfortable and anxious to get the few miles into town.

We all three tried to just calmly talk to the two in the front seat when, suddenly, the front seat passenger, pulls a huge .45 caliber pistol from under his seat, and says "What do you f--kers think about this cannon?" I was in the middle of the back seat, and I have never seen such a large bore weapon staring me in the face. All I could say, stuttering badly, was "that's quite a gun, would you point that somewhere else?" His eyes were not fluttering now as his face turned red with rage and screamed "F-ck no! How about I just blow you away, asshole?"

I now couldn't say anything, just shook my head, no. My friends said nothing. The driver decided it was time to race on the highway. Maybe this was the race to "kick some ass," maybe our asses.

We were probably going 90-100 mph, passing other cars, but all I could see was that huge pistol with the huge bore hole so close to my face. It was wobbling around. When he cocked the hammer I really believed this could be it. End of story, in the back seat of a car with two stoners out to have some violent fun.

The pistol holder put his eye down to sight the gun right at my mouth, and slurring his words, said, "You think I'm kidding?" I just shook my head, no. He laughed or I should say it was more like a cackle, and then his mouth opened wide, and I focused on the missing teeth. There appeared to be more gone than were still in there, and he was so young. I found myself thinking incredibly, "how could he be so young and have so few teeth. I wonder if he has ever seen a dentist. I wonder if he will be able to keep the few he has left. They don't look so good. I caught myself with "What am I thinking"? Why am I thinking about his teeth when he's just about to kill me? I thought about my wife and family. This is better, I thought. This is what I should be thinking about. Will they be OK? Will my friends be OK?

Then, this idiot starts pretending to cry as he says "you know I'm going to miss you so much – and I don't even know you! Ha"

My mind then seemed to go blank as his buddy slows the car down, and time itself seemed to go into slow motion as my gun-pointing amigo turns to his driver friend and say "Why are you slowing down, you Dick?"

The driver says "F-ck you" and keeps slowing down as we came to a red light (according to what my friends told me later). We stopped at the light, the guy with the gun turned it toward the driver and I came out of my dazed condition and yelled to my friends "Get out!" We all three jumped out and took off running. The two last things I heard were local knuckleheads laughing and the roar of their car as they ran the red light and screamed on down the road.

At the side of the road, we tried to pull ourselves together, but that wasn't so easy. I couldn't believe what just happened to us. After a few minutes, we walked the rest of the way into Leesville. One guy in a pick-up truck stopped and offered us a ride. We declined.

When we finally got to Leesville, all we saw were bars, strip-club bars and fast food joints. We had some fast food, drank a beer at a sleepy bar, and went to a movie.

We took the bus back to Ft. Polk. I only went back into Leesville one other time during my AIT training – with about 10 other friends, riding the bus, going to a pizza joint, then went back to the base. What a waste.

C-4

C-4 is a very powerful explosive that was demonstrated for us in a weapons class. It can be formed into various shapes from brick form to corded-rope–form. The trainers wrapped a 1"-2" cord around a pine tree and blew it up. The tree, in an explosion of bark and branches, fell over with a loud crash. We were impressed. No samples were passed out. We just watched. That was fine with me.

Live Fire

One night- training session involved low crawling (crawling tight to the ground on your belly) under what was claimed to be live machine-gun fire over our heads. We were told, "If you panic and stand up – you're dead." I doubted it was real.

There I was crawling over the wet, muddy ground and screaming over our heads were tracer rounds. It was real. No-one stood up. We crawled and we crawled without incident – other than fear –no it was terror. I couldn't believe they would really fire live rounds right over our heads. It happened.

"Expert" Rifleman

AIT is supposedly where we were to get advanced training in weapons, how to fight in the jungle, and develop our warrior skills. Great, I want to learn how to be a more effective killer. "Rambo" me, as quickly as possible. I want to go to war. I want to free South Vietnam from the Communist menace from the north.

Let's learn how to shoot straight, and survive in a hostile country where the "bad guys" wear funny pointed bamboo hats. Let's blow up kids in tunnels in the ground who want to kill you in your sleep.

The AIT training NCO's (Non-commissioned officers – Sergeants largely) were mainly soldiers back from Vietnam – usually combat veterans, not support personnel away from the "action." As a group, these soldiers were surly, aged for their chronological years, and not happy to be working with a bunch of "greenhorns" who were probably going to go thousands of miles away and come back in body bags if they have any pieces left to bring back at all.

So often we heard statements from these combat veterans like "Kiss your ass good-by," "Charlie will blow your shit away," "You're a dead man walking," "Keep your spacing – one round (mortar) will kill you all, and "Those gooks will blow you away," and "you shits are fu—ked."

If they were trying to scare us, I would have to say it worked. Even though I was counting on not visiting Southeast Asia, most of those around me were expecting to. Slowly, the "John Wayne" bravado was eroding, replaced with disillusionment – and fear.

The most believable trainers were not the loud screamers, but the quiet ones – the ones who would say with what looked to be dead eyes "I'll tell you what it's really like and you can listen or not listen, I really don't give a shit." Then, they would tell us how to look for trip wires (booby traps), Bouncing Betty" anti-personnel mines set throughout the jungle, usually on the trails U.S. soldiers traversed. The Betty's, when stepped on would jump up, explode at about the height of a man's groin area. Not always meant to kill, but to maim.

We were told the Viet Cong viewed the war as a war of attrition. Cause injuries which require many support personnel to care for the casualties. As all other "invaders," eventually, the U.S. would leave. In fact, this is exactly what happened.

The more reluctant these combat veterans were to tell stories, the more believable were the stories themselves. I saw many of these young men as damaged, many severely so.

We often went to the firing range to endlessly fire M-16's. This weapon was designed for putting out lots of firepower in close-combat situations. E.g., jungle environments. What we quickly learned was how rapidly this weapon got dirty firing so many shells, and how quickly it seemed to jam (I've been told subsequent improvements in design have helped with this problem). The M-16 could be set to fire in auto mode (continuous firing) or semi-mode (one shot at a time). It didn't matter which mode I used, I was a terrible shot.

The day of "Qualification," meaning a rifle range test of our ability to shoot accurately arrived and off we marched to the shooting range which had targets at different distances (100 yards, 200 yards, 500 yards). Each range position (foxhole) had an evaluator with binoculars and score sheet on a clipboard.

Over the loudspeaker we heard our instructions of when to fire, how often, and when to cease fire for a change in targets and distances. I did give my best effort. After firing 10 clips of ammo, I asked my evaluator how I did. "Oh great", he said, "You hit the target in the shooting lane to the right and left a few times. Not much damage to your targets." He smiled a little bit. "I'm not surprised" I said. "Don't worry" he said, "I think you're an expert." "What?" I said, that's crazy." "It sure is", he said and smiled again.

The next day, in formation, about half the platoon was called up front and awarded an "Expert" badge to wear on our uniforms. Explain that! I was so proud?

I did get an explanation later. The Army required every company to qualify at least half of its soldiers as "Expert Riflemen." There you have it.

Gas Attack

As part of the training for possible exposure to gas warfare, we had to practice putting our gas masks on as fast as we could. Then we had to, in groups of 10, go into a tear gas room (actually called CS. I never knew what that stood for) wearing our gas masks, then remove them in the room, and fumble to get them back on. Very unpleasant, but the Army was making a point. Be ready.

At random times out in the field, the Training Sergeant would yell "Gas! Gas!" and we had to put on our masks – again as fast as we could. To make it more realistic, an occasional canister of CS was popped and thrown in our midst. It's amazing how strong this gas was as it made your skin feel like it was on fire, with lots of tears and coughing. Nasty stuff. We all felt ill for hours, coughing and trying to clear our vision.

The trainers often claimed our gas masks were also to be used in case of nuclear exposure. I found out later these particular masks would help very little if at all. I guess it was supposed to make us feel better. It didn't.

Grenades

Part of AIT training included the proper care and feeding of hand grenades. Clearly dangerous, yes. We attended a class on the destructive capabilities of this weapon, and how we were to handle it and how to throw it.

But, only on the firing line could you feel the weight, practice throwing and experience the attendant anxiety. The firing line included long trenches that looked right out of a World War I movie. The Training Sergeants were, understandably, a nervous lot. I was in the trench, and handed a live grenade with a sergeant who showed an obvious nervous tic in his right eye, alternating squinting and rapidly blinking. The left eye just remained open and I never noticed it blinking at all. I think he'd been on the firing line too long.

He kept repeating to me – over and over again "Hold this tight in your throwing hand, covering the handle. Got it? Got it?" I was holding it correctly, I guess, but he repeated again "Got it? Got it?" " I got it sergeant," I said. "Shut up" he said, and then he went on "Now pull out the pin and throw this baby downrange as far as you can. Do not drop it! You hear me? Don't drop it you dummy." "I won't", I said.

I pulled the pin and threw it – hard – downrange as the sergeant was again screaming "Now Get Down!" "Get Down." I did. You could hear the shrapnel fragments ringing in the air. The explosion was so much louder than I expected. We stood and he slapped me across the helmet and said "Now get the hell out of here." I did.

The next practice times were easier, but the trainers were no less anxious. What a job they had.

Napalm

Our entire company was trucked out to a bombing range, miles from Ft. Polk. We were to witness the effects of napalm-jellied gas dropped from fighter jets. This weapon was used often in Vietnam to clear enemy positions. In jelly form, the ignited gas would spread across the target area burning anything exposed.

A fighter screamed over our heads, and dropped the napalm. It was the most horrific thing I had ever witnessed. I can't imagine what this would do to its victims, even though I've seen pictures and film about the bombing in Vietnam. It looked like a picture of hell. I threw up.

I understand a form of napalm goes back to usage in World War II, particularly against Germany. Nasty stuff.

Survival Course

The AIT training included what was labeled an Escape and Evasion Course (E&E – remember the Army acronyms?) or survival course.

The course was held in the Louisiana swamps and was designed to include a simulated Viet Cong base with U.S. Army personnel playing the role of interrogators of captured prisoners. They wore the clothing of Viet Cong, and exposed captured U.S. soldiers to "simulated" torture in a simulated prison camp. As demonstrated to us before the exercise began, the simulations were pretty hard on the prisoners, and the prisoners verified the abuse after the all-night exercise.

Basically, we were released, at dark, at the beginning of the jungle course and had to traverse about 5 miles through the swamps, without being caught by the Viet Cong. We were given a map, compass and repeatedly told "don't get caught!" We had no food or water, and we were expected to find the rally point designated miles from the start, by daylight the next morning.

It was a formidable course, with rifle fire throughout the jungle. Illumination flares shot up into the very dark night, and occasional screaming coming from somewhere in the jungle at the "Viet- Cong camp." It was very, very realistic, and terror provoking.

I was released into the course with two friends I had made in AIT, one an attorney, and the other a graduate student at the University of Texas.

We entered the woods, found a place to huddle together, and planned what we were gong to do. In looking at the maps, the attorney had an interesting suggestion. "Look at this road here – it's out of bounds and I know we have been warned that if we try to cross the road and go out of bounds we will be court-martialed, and recycled to repeat AIT, but it might be worth the risk." I added "You know, this is an evasion course and they tell us to use our wits and skills like we were in a war zone, so why not give it a try? I sure don't want to be caught by those crazy interrogators." The UT student expressed his concern that "the last thing I want to do is repeat AIT." "Enough discussion," I said, "I'm in." The other two agreed.

We studied the map, and decided where to try to cross the road (patrolled by "enemy" jeeps). It was scary, but after sneaking through the woods for over an hour, we managed to cross the road. Farther into the woods we went, and walked the 4+ miles to near the course end-point. There, we hid for most of the rest of the night, and, near dawn, were able to cross back into the course, and acting completely bedraggled and worn-out, entered the rally point.

Heartily congratulated by the Training Sergeants we got plenty to eat and drink. "Man, that was a rough course" I told one grizzled sergeant dressed like a Viet Cong. "You bet it is "he said. "I hope you learned something." "Sure did, sergeant," I replied.

The three of us never told a soul. That would have meant big trouble. Some of the captured soldiers were "roughed- up" pretty badly. I'm not convinced recruits could be treated that way in today's Army. At least I hope not.

Ambush

In preparation for those bound for the war in Vietnam, jungle ambush training was frequently on our schedule. In the daylight hours, we would practice setting up ambushes in what were expected to be very much like the trails in Vietnam. We were schooled in camouflage and fields of fire, and setting up land-mines. This always involved lots of grumbling about lying in hidden positions for hours without moving, or making noise of any kind. So, if the grumbling was audible, it was quickly responded to by the training personnel. I would hear angry whispers from the sergeant at a nearby position that sounded like "Just what the f---k are you doing, you stupid and soon-to-be dead soldier? Shut up! Don't even make a noise, even if you have to piss your pants!"

The night ambush training was always dreaded. Walking through water to get to the ambush site in daytime, where you could splash the water when you saw a water moccasin (Cottonmouth) was one thing, but walking the swamps at night when you could see nothing was very different. We were told so often how aggressive Cottonmouths were, but what do you do when you can't even see the water you're walking through? All I could do was hope they weren't where I was walking. I did try to splash the water some, but would usually hear a sergeant say "Shut-up," through the darkness. I would think to myself "If I get stuck in Vietnam, I'll be real quiet there, but here I'm going to make a little water noise. Once, a trainer grabbed my backpack and hissed "is that you puke?" "No," I whispered back.

If we were going to spend several hours in ambush positions, the silence of the night was occasionally punctuated with "AAAHHHH," and rustling or even running in the woods. At daylight, when we moved out we would get the story, - usually a soldier visited by a snake or scorpion. Unnerving and all-too-realistic.

Overnight marches and campouts were also interesting. For example, if you took your boots off to sleep (many of us didn't remove them) in your sleeping bag, you had to cover your boots with a pair of socks. Unfriendly critters would often take up residence in boots (or sleeping bags) overnight. I never got used to the variety of insects, often huge and nasty critters in the jungle.

The mosquitoes were, all told, the worst. Their incessant attacks were more than an irritant, and they were, at times, intolerable. And, the Army-issued-repellant was almost as bad as the mosquitoes. I often wondered just what was in that repellant. It burned the skin, and if you got it even near a cut or your eyes, it was very, very unpleasant. Some of the larger species of mosquitoes seemed to be attracted to the exposed parts of your body where I applied the repellant. How could that be? My imagination?

I remember one soldier from New York was stung by a scorpion, panicked, threw his rifle and pack down and took off running through the woods. The scorpion sting was minor, but the broken leg he got from the panic, running, and crashing in a ditch wasn't.

The first time I saw a soldier bitten by a snake, I thought it killed him. It didn't, he just passed out and was taken out of the woods by a medivac helicopter. Those helicopter pilots were amazing. They could land in a site that looked too small to park a Volkswagen (a slight exaggeration). The injured soldier returned two days later. He loved showing off his snakebite puncture wounds.

Firing Range

In AIT we spent hours on various firing ranges. I couldn't even estimate the amount of ammunition I burned up on those ranges, much less, all of us together.

Some soldiers, during all this training were marginal psychologically, and a few just emotionally and behaviorally crashed. On the M-16 firing range, one soldier "lost it" while lying prone (on his stomach), after a range sergeant kicked him in the rear end. The young man screamed, and was scrambling to his feet and turning his rifle on the sergeant when he was tackled by two other soldiers.

It was a scary sight. I never saw that young man again after he was taken away. Our platoon sergeant wouldn't tell us what happened to him.

I'm Bad

Barely old enough to vote. Talking big about "winning the war." Loud enough to consistently draw attention to himself. Telling any-and-everyone what a "badass" he is. Seeking a way to pick a fight with those smaller than himself. Interminably complaining about how long it takes with this "baby training." "I'm ready to go now! Let's get it on."

On and on he talked, excited about getting to the rifle range to practice shooting some bad guys. "I'm ready! Are you guys ready? Let's get some."

Randy was a classic immature young man (boy), barely educated, and had difficultly reading, including letters from his girlfriend back home in Mississippi (a fifteen-year-old girl).

Over the first two weeks of AIT training his relentless mouth droned on , to the irritation of virtually everyone around him. Late one Saturday evening, after coming in from the field where we were training in map-reading, Randy made a big mistake. He popped off with a racial slur to one of the African-American "Brothers." To a rather diminutive Black man tuning his radio, Randy said "Hey there you cannibal, get the fried chicken out of your ears and put on some real music."

Within five minutes, Randy was surrounded by six unhappy looking Brothers who asked those of us "White Boys" close by to give them a little time to talk with Randy. We did. No one felt the need to help this loud-mouth.

Randy went on sick-call the next morning after a long night of moaning piteously in his bunk. Two days later he returned to the barracks with a much subdued demeanor. His complaints to the training sergeants were ignored.

Canines

During AIT we occasionally heard stories about the use of dogs in the Vietnam War. During one class on map-reading, our instructor told us he was, for a while, part of a program using canines, in particular German Shepherds, in the jungles of Vietnam. He described their use with the "point man" on patrols because the dogs could hear/detect the presence of enemy soldiers before a human could. Especially helpful was being aware of a warning for walking into a trap or "kill-zone."

He told us he left this specialized part of the Army because he "lost too many animals." Dogs, like humans, could trigger land mines.

It seems that, like the soldiers themselves, these dogs would often not come back, or came back damaged – like the soldiers themselves. What did they do with the survivors?

Parade

Everybody loves a parade. Well, almost everybody. I used to enjoy parades, until I had to be in one, all dressed up in my "Class A's" dress uniform. All for show, you see a general was visiting Fort Polk to assess training programs. So, naturally there needed to be a parade of trainees. The one good thing about it was we missed a half-day of field training.

We got our boots shined to an even brighter gloss, shined our copper belt buckles with Brasso, gave ourselves a fresh shave, and marched out to the parade grounds to practice, again, marching by the review stand. We were awful. It seemed the more we practiced, the worse we got. Especially with everyone keeping in step, keeping the proper spacing from each other, and quickly turning our eyes to the right on command when we were even with "General Whoever."

If the practice was bad, the actual "performance" was worse. About the time we were level with General "Patton" I noticed we looked like what the German army looked like in the
WWII retreat from the Battle of Stalingrad.

Our company officers and trainers were not happy, to not put a fine point on it.

After the parade festivities we were scolded in no uncertain terms from sergeants up to the company commander. Among other descriptors, we were "the worst bunch of lazy, lousy soldiers the U.S. Army ever produced."

After the rest of the day spent in regular training we were taken back out to the parade grounds, under the lights, to "practice til we get it right." About 4:30 a.m. everybody gave up and we went back to the barracks and bed, for about an hour before we got up to return to the regular training routine.

My explanation was fairly simple. We hadn't had any parade marches since Basic Training and you forget what you don't often practice. Like keeping separate your left versus your right foot.

Band of Brothers

What a fabulous movie. Band of Brothers starring Tom Hanks that was released many years ago was incredible in terms of portraying the complicated relationships emerging among men during the horrors of World War II. I wish I could say I thought some of that camaraderie, loyalty, and sacrifice for your fellow soldier/brother was present in my time in the military. But, it simply wasn't there. Could that be because of whom I was then? Could it be that kind of brotherhood is only present in the confusion, sacrifice, and terror of combat? Could our culture have changed such that relationships are now less likely? Could the characteristics of warfare have changed such that technological warfare is replacing the personal up close aspects of fighting and dying? Could military training methods have so changed to reduce the emergence of brotherhood? Could it be something else, or a combination of "something elses?"

I experienced only fleeting examples of the development of unit cohesion, comradeship, teamwork, and commitment to the welfare of our fellow soldiers. Instead, I saw, most often, self-centeredness, self-protection, "just get through this" attitude, without an over-reaching regard for those around us. Why? I can only speculate.

One thought that often rattled around in my head had to do with one of the overall motives that permeated our training. It seemed the emphasis was on personal survival rather than on the objectives or even the need for the mission – that being the Vietnam War. The closest we got to the team-building was "Just do your job, keep your head down stupid, too bad you have to go to the Vietnam shit." Occasionally, say on a long march or run, I would see someone "fall out," that is quit marching or running, pass out from the heat or fatigue, and another soldier stop to help. This invariably led to the training sergeant screaming at the assisting soldier "Just keep up! Let the medics deal with that pussy!"

I didn't see this as building "team cohesion" or "we never leave anyone behind" or any of the other trite exclamations seen in movies.

In sum, the attitude taught was more "put in your time and go home." I believed this was, in part, due to the total helplessness and unpopularity of the whole Vietnam conflict.

Imagine

Untold numbers of times during training, I had the question reverberating through my mind "what if I had to go into a war- a real combat situation with these men around me? How would I do? How would my fellow soldiers do? Would I be so afraid I'd freeze? Could I be a coward? Run even? Could I trust those next to me? Could they trust me? What if something happened to me? What if I saw a friend hurt or killed?"

I clearly knew I was questioning this whole Vietnam misadventure. I believe this was a war without the possibility of "winning." I believed the goal of "winning the heart and minds of the Vietnamese people" was ridiculous – especially since we were killing so many of them. I didn't believe we knew what was best for a people so far away and so different from us. I didn't believe our security as a nation depended on "defeating the North Vietnamese communists." I didn't believe we were being told the truth, as a nation, about how the war was being conducted, how we treated civilians, even how we treated "the enemy." I didn't even have a clear understanding of why they were our "enemy." What made them that?

I didn't believe our trainers who would tell us the evils of the "communist gooks" trying to take away the freedoms of a helpless country of poor peasants.

I did believe the returning Vets who were telling us things when out of the view of the majority of the staff. Things like:

Keep your head down.

Keep your rifle clean – they jam.

Don't trust a fresh Louie (new 2nd Lieutenant).

That's a beautiful country if it wasn't for the heat, the bugs, and the war.

You'll be lucky if you don't get your shit blown away.

You poor suckers.

Just mind your own business.

Don't volunteer for nothing.

Stay away from people you don't know.

Heroes die.

But, the Vets who told us the most, said nothing, and wouldn't talk about it – at all.

More School

This is a sad story – at least for me. As we got within about two weeks of the end of AIT, we all knew our next orders were coming soon. Most of the draftees were going on a long trip – to Vietnam. So, the Army made an interesting offer. If you will sign up to extend your enlistment from two years to four (or five in a few cases) you can go to another school (and postpone Vietnam). Examples of another school could be Military Police (MP), or Intelligence, Aircraft Repair, or Officer Candidate School (for a select few). Sadly some, especially those so scared about going to Vietnam, agreed to this extension.

What a price to pay for a little more time. The Vietnam War was to go on for years. My hope is a few of those young men didn't have to end up going after all. Most of them did go. Only some returned whole.

Religion

The military was very good about providing opportunities for those of religious faith or beliefs to worship. On many Sundays religious services were available for the faiths represented by Protestants, Catholics and Jewish persuasions. I never saw services for Muslims. It must be remembered that this was before the dramatic growth of the number of Muslims in the U.S. (and worldwide). There was, however, a "chapel" for those who wished to worship as they wished by themselves.

Overall, it was my observation that less than 10% of the soldiers I trained with in Basic or AIT availed themselves of worship opportunities provided by the Army.

This changed dramatically as AIT training came to an end, and orders were "cut" for the next assignment. That next assignment for most was, of course, Vietnam. The closer we got to training ending, the greater the interest in issues of faith.

I recall the old adage "there are no atheists in foxholes." I don't know about that, but I saw many young men thinking more about their own mortality as they faced the reality of war in a far distant place. Personal consults with chaplains became much more frequent at this time as well. A few soldiers rather suddenly decided they were Conscientious Objectors (CO's). The Army was not sympathetic to these late conversions. This was sad to see.

Chapter 4: Airborne School

Right after AIT at lovely Ft. Polk, I was assigned to Ft. Benning, Georgia for 3 weeks of Airborne School. I was ready for a change – to leave Ft. Polk and the beauty of the primitive woods to find civilization. Three more weeks. I can do that. Really, I'm almost home, right? What new can happen to me in 3 short weeks? Then, I made another big mistake. I started thinking more about what could happen. Jumping out of a perfectly good airplane. How dumb is that?

Jump School

I'm on my way to Ft. Benning, Georgia for Jump School. It's still hard to believe I "volunteered" (I view it as under the duress of being drafted) to jump out of a functioning airplane.

The use of paratroopers in combat has a checkered history, which I will not review in detail here. Suffice it to say dropping troops from the sky has had some spectacular successes, as well as some horrific failures. Same conclusion with rescue missions using paratroopers.

In my view, current day use of paratroopers is largely unnecessary, and outdated, especially with the availability of various types of helicopters. It has become more of a status symbol than a military necessity, and an avenue to accelerate rank and grade advancement.

By its very nature, parachute jumps are dangerous, with frequent injuries and some fatalities. So much can go wrong, including: unfavorable weather conditions (and winds, especially, if over 10-12 mph), faulty equipment (including the jump planes and helicopters as well as problems with the parachute and related gear), poor pilot/navigator decisions about when exactly to begin the jump, and other military decisions about when and where to jump (e.g. drop-zone location).

Jump school was not for the faint of heart. The dropout rate was high (In my class 30%), and a number were "recycled." This meant sent back to start the 3 week training again. Recycling could be because of disciplinary problems, inadequate physical readiness, illness, injury, or a myriad of other reasons. It was frequently used by the trainers as a form of intimidation (motivation. "I'm going to recycle your punk ass if you don't…").

The trainers were a special breed. They were called "Black Hats" for the distinctive black baseball caps they wore. Mainly non-commissioned officers, these sergeants were the most unpleasant individuals I met in my entire 6 years in the Army. They were obnoxious, vulgar, loud (very), and ….mean! They probably also represented the most professional and best training I experienced.

Jump School lasted 3 weeks, at a minimum. It seemed so much longer.

Week 1: Hell week. Incredible physical training and more running than I had been exposed to, to-date.

Some classes were also started in a limited way, in how to land, positioning and exiting the aircraft, care of equipment, etc.

Week 2: Tower Week – a 300 foot tower with pre-attached and opened parachutes would lift off from the ground with a paratrooper hooked into a jump harness and raised to a height of 300 feet and released. This was to practice the PLF (Parachute Landing Fall). The ground was a pre-plowed, soft soil to reduce injuries as we were learning just how to land and roll our body upon impact. Even in this partially protected environment, injuries happened. Again, equipment failure and "operator error" – us students. I must say, I paid close attention during these 3 weeks. Much more so than before. The classes were more intense, and much more detailed.

Week 3: Jump Week we had more physical training, classes, but this was the week we actually exited an aircraft flying 2000 ft + in the air. The first training aircraft we used was a C-119 troop transport. It held about 22 jumpers and was a two propeller, old, loud craft that vibrated like a cheap hotel vibrating bed. At our first jump we taxied to the end of the runway after a long wait "in harness" checking equipment and being totally terrified. Some soldiers wet and or soiled their fatigues. A few talked a good game of bravado but most of us were very quiet.

The testosterone present was ubiquitous. Getting ready for our first real test – the first jump during Jump Week. There were the loud ones, proclaiming "finally we get to do this – to jump for real. Not from mock plane doors or a 300 foot tower on a soft landing field!" There were the quiet ones, not saying much, if anything at all. When asked if they were ready, they would merely nod or say something like "I'm OK."

Most of us were somewhere in between. Talking some, playing the "I'm tough" game but secretly knowing it was just talk. It was just talk because the fear was real, palpable, and growing, the closer we got to jump time. In my own head, I'm thinking "Is this for real? Am I really going to go up in the air and jump from a functioning plane?"

Fear

The fear was real, pervasive, and contagious. The closer to boarding the plane, the quieter it became, even for the loud-mouths. Finally, we boarded, sat down in nylon-crowded harnesses, and the steely voices of the training sergeants took over. "Now ladies, listen up. You will not be afraid, you will not throw up (some did), you will not hesitate in the door, cause if you do, you will get my boot up your ass, and I don't want to lose my boot ---again! Got it?" "We just looked at him. He had more to say. "Our flight time is 35 minutes, there will be no in-flight meal" (he smiled), "no magazines and no fear. Are we clear? You will do your job. You're going to love it" (another smile). "Use your training and you'll probably live – till you get to the Nam" (no smile here).

Heart racing, perspiring even though it was cold in the plane, hands slightly trembling I went out into the rushing wind. No one on our plane hesitated at the door, and all survived the first jump with only one broken leg and a few bumps and scrapes.

Second jump. I had never known fear like this. Eventually, my mind went into neutral, just focusing on what my training taught me to do. A couple more soldiers threw up. That was also, not any longer unusual. Now, sitting in very cramped nylon strap seats we hear the engines rev even higher and louder, and with greater vibration. How can this thing hold together? Finally, we lurch forward, and it seems as if it takes forever to get airborne. Compared with modern airplanes, this is an antique. We circle around, climbing higher until we're at the proper altitude and approaching the drop-zone – a huge field surrounded by forest. Just like in the movies the Jumpmaster (Sergeant in charge of getting us out the door) yells "Stand up," then, "Hook up" (attach our static line to the cable running above us the length of the seating area), then "Check Equipment" during which we check to see that the jumper in front of us has his static line properly attached to the cable above us, the "Prepare to Jump" (I never was clear about what exactly that meant we were supposed to do except get more scared), then the light at the front of the bulkhead would change from red to green and the jumpmaster would yell "Jump! Jump! Jump!" We would file forward, jamming into the man in front of us, approaching the door (one on each side of the plane), grab the sides of the exit opening and leap out. If you were lucky, after a few feet of free-fall, the end of the static line would be reached, your feet would snap forward and the parachute would begin to open as you fell toward the ground. I would then look up, to see if, in fact, the parachute was deploying. If it was a good opening, fully deployed and not tangled with another trooper, or completely tangled within itself (a "cigarette roll"), I would look at the ground and if need be, pull on the risers (straps holding the parachute) to avoid other jumpers. If we were headed toward another parachutist's lines, we were to extend both arms and hands to, hopefully, bounce off and not go through his lines and become tangled. When lines are crossed, you "steal air" from the other trooper, and both descend and land too fast – hence more injuries. So, I would do what steering I could in the air to void other soldiers, and to not land on anyone, or anything else.

If the parachute failed to deploy, we were to pull the reserve chute handle attached to the front of our harness on our chest. It was a small parachute, but we were happy to have them.

I landed successfully, gave a whoop, released my parachute from my harness, got out of the harness, gathered my chute in a ball and ran to the field sites marked for our company. Coming down, I can remember how quickly the ground approached, and how quiet it was in the air. Eerily quiet, especially once the planes had flown over.

Oh so glad to be back on the ground, and in one piece!

That night was a happy night in the barracks. Lots of beer, lots of pizza. The "Black Hats" even left us alone – until the next morning with the rude wake up at 5:00 a.m. to get ready to jump again. In our company we had only two injuries – a broken leg and a concussion. Very fortunate to just have two, but, sadly after recovery, they would have to start the training all over.

I had more jumps that week, without injury, and looked forward to Graduation Day on Friday of the third and final week.

I really was proud of surviving and getting my Jump Wings pinned on my chest during the ceremony. Next – going home! Two days later, I flew to home to my wife and family. Happy Day.

C-141

The huge C-141 airplane was a challenge. The large door at the rear of the plane would be lowered when it was time to exit and we didn't really jump out, we just walked off the huge door. The advantage was we could exit more quickly, but the disadvantage was the tremendous jet engine prop blast that would hit us. I always thought the increased turbulence came from this huge plane's inability to fly slowly enough to minimize the blast. Regardless, we had frequent tangled lines from our parachutes.

I had an officer come flying through my lines because he formed into a ball instead of splaying his arms and legs as all of us were trained to do. So, we were tangled together, going down way too fast. There he was about 8 feet above me as we descended, stealing my air, deflating my parachute when, incredibly, he unstrapped his K-Bar knife from his leg and began cutting my lines.

I began screaming things that I didn't know I had in me. He stopped cutting my lines. Then we hit hard on the ground. I went after this lousy officer and I won't tell what I did to him, but when the higher-ups heard the whole story, I was not reprimanded. The unit commander told me "Let's just drop this whole thing, OK soldier?" I said, "Under one condition – keep that Lieutenant away from me." The Captain thought that was a good idea – as he said "Agreed."

Equipment Jump

Exiting aircraft with a full complement of equipment was not what most of us considered fun. Wearing a heavy steel- pot (helmet), M-16, magazines of ammo, camping gear and all that included always meant a more crowded aircraft, waddling to board, waddling to jump out the exit doors, and what always seemed like a faster descent.

On one equipment jump, the soldier in front of me got to the exit door, and froze. He hesitated, holding the sides of the door and wouldn't jump out. The Jumpmaster standing in the door grabbed him by his bulky equipment and literally threw him out the door with colorful expletives.

On a later equipment jump, one soldier had a four foot box containing an M-60 heavy machine gun attached by a 6 ft nylon cord to his leg. The box was shoved out the door and the soldier was to jump out quickly following it. The machine -gun box went out, pulled the strap on his leg, which snapped (the strap). The trooper looked astonished as he hesitated in the door. Again, the Jumpmaster shoved him out screaming "Go get it you moron!" I just had to laugh, ever so briefly as I scrambled out next. Fortunately, the very heavy machine-gun box did not land on anyone. Any victim it hit would not have survived.

One equipment jump was an absolute disaster. This particular jump included dropping multiple heavy cargo boxes of mortars, munitions, food and water supplies, tents, small artillery, and 3 jeeps. The heavier equipment had more than one parachute attached.

What made this jump a disaster was timing. The troopers from 15 airplanes exited and were just landing on the drop-zone when I saw and heard sergeants and officers running across the drop zone yelling up to us "Abandon your chutes and get off the drop-zone. Do not gather your parachutes. Get off the drop-zone! Now!"

When I looked up into the sky, I saw why all the hysterics. The equipment from other planes was overhead and coming down on us. The timing for the equipment drop was early. By some miracle, no one was crushed to death, but we were a very hostile group of soldiers once we cleared the drop-zone! FUBAR!*

*Fu--ked up beyond all recognition

Combat Jumps

Infrequently, we had what were called Combat Jumps. This only meant low altitude jumps – 1,000 ft, sometimes 900 ft. To put it simply, if your chute doesn't deploy immediately and fully, you'd better pull your reserve parachute ASAP.

Combine a combat jump with a full equipment complement and it's even more exciting.

Now combine a combat jump with all our equipment, and do it at night and that means even more enjoyment. Pure terror.

No, It's Not Cold

The weather was turning cold in Georgia. The mornings arrived with frost on the ground, on all our equipment and parachute harnesses with all the metal clips. But, winter coats were not allowed. Not at all. Each morning we gathered for "formation" roll call, and the physical training (PT) would begin. Breakfast awaited a solid hour of P.T. There we were shivering, complaining (to ourselves) wondering why we couldn't just put on our OD (Olive Drab of course) coats sitting there unused in our lockers.

Finally, one extra cold morning, one brave (foolish) trainee couldn't help himself. He asked a "Black Hat" Training Sergeant. "Sarge, can we get our coats on- - it's cold." The Black Hat, in a purple rage, literally ran over to the trainee, screaming a truly creative list of expletives at 120 decibels, at least, and the trainee was a regular army colonel. The tirade included descriptions such as "you maggot, you turd, you ignorant poor excuse for a human being", plus more crudities interspersed. All 1/2 inch from the colonel's nose. After all this, the Black Hat said "Sir, I'm going to answer your stupid question even though you don't deserve an answer. You cannot wear a coat for two simple reasons. So simple maybe even you can understand them. Number one: no coat because the

Army says it's not cold, got it numbnuts?" The officer paled, but the Black Hat wasn't finished. " Number two: the Army says it's not winter yet! Maybe this will warm you up pretty baby—get down and give me twenty push-ups! Sir."

There were no more questions, much less complaints about the cold.

You Will Not Be Afraid

We heard this order frequently in Airborne School. For example, "You're going to jump out of this 300 ft. tower and you will not be afraid."

"You're going to jump out of that C-119 trainer, keep your eyes open, guide your chute to the middle of the L Z, conduct a perfect PLF (Parachute Landing Fall) on the ground, jump up, un-harness, roll your chute, and run off the L Z and you will not be afraid.

"If you think you're afraid of jumping out of that fine aircraft, don't think! You will not be afraid."

Onboard the airplane our jump-master yells "You are ordered to not be afraid. I repeat, you will not be afraid! You will not even think about being afraid." (Who brought this subject up?) "If you even think about being afraid, I will rip your head off and shit down your neck" (Nice thought). "Think about that, but not about being afraid." You are, for the duration of this jump, to not be afraid. "If you think you're going to be afraid, don't do it! I would tell you if you could be afraid, and I'm not going to tell you you can – so don't be! "Don't even think about thinking of being afraid (what?)" "If you're afraid, you don't belong in my Army. And since you're here in my Army you must not be afraid – ever. Just don't." (Uh, could you go over that again?).

"If you think about anything, doubts will come into your ignorant heads. So don't think! Don't think at all and you won't know fear." A few minutes later, the same Jumpmaster tells us as we're boarding the plane, "now think about your landing, the wind direction, and how to untangle if you get stuck in another jumper's parachute lines" (What happened to don't think?).

"Fear does not exist in the U.S. Army. The worst thing that can happen is that you die. So what? You will not be afraid. You will not piss your pants on this jump. You will not shit your pants. You will be men. You will not be afraid. If you die, die like a man – with no fear. You're not worth anything anyway! Am I right? Am I right? Damn right, I'm right" (Not really).

"If you're afraid, I'm going to kill you. Be afraid of that."

So much talk of fear. It seemed the more we were told to not be afraid, the more fear was generated. The more we were told to not think of being afraid, the more we thought about it. Same old story. How can you be told not to think about something, and not?

The Army had a lot of difficultly differentiating between the complex phenomena of experiencing fear, versus showing fear. Or, worse yet, for the mission at hand, showing fear that hinders doing your job.

We all experience fear. It's how to cope with this normal emotion that can be worked with, managed to some degree, and develop coping mechanisms when fear is present.

In sum, the lack of thinking or unproductive thinking often trickles down from the top.

Finally, Airborne School is over and I'm heading home. That was the longest three weeks in my life. Now, I'm facing 5 1/2 years of Texas Airborne Army National Guard service, including monthly weekend meetings and annual summer camps for two weeks. I hope our unit doesn't get called up for active duty and we end up in Vietnam despite my efforts to stay in graduate school. It's a gamble. Many other National Guard units across the U.S. have been activated for this interminable war. It could happen to us – and me. I can only hope not.

Chapter 5: Summer Camp

So, each summer our National Guard unit, in its entirety, would pack up all our gear and head out for two weeks plus. The destination varied from year to year, but most often we were bound for Ft. Hood, Texas, or bases in Colorado.

I often wondered who or why the destination choices we arrived at were chosen, but clearly, this was not within my purview to know. Our local cadre of officers and sergeants took great pride in finding out the destination but keeping it a national security secret. They never seemed to figure out we didn't care, because the summer camps were so much the same.

No matter where you go, there you are. Here are some highlights of our annual vacations.

Maneuvers

This is an interesting word – "maneuvers." We heard this a lot in training and in our summer camps. "Men, today we're going on maneuvers," says our company 1st Lieutenant (the second lowest ranking officer).

What this information meant to me was the following: Our whole company of about 120 men consisting of 4 platoons of about 30 men each, would pack up all our camping gear, march out to the woods and dirt fields of Ft. Hood, Texas, and wander around. After "maneuvering" around we would sit down, usually for hours at a time, and fight the mosquitoes. The officers would run around excitedly talking on their radios (when they worked), giving orders to the sergeants who would give orders to us that usually went like "OK men prepare to…." We were always preparing to do something. Something like "prepare to move out" or "prepare to gear up" or "prepare to march" or "prepare to maneuver to Point Charlie." To me, "prepare to" meant just sit on your rear because nothing is happening anytime soon. I loved it. If something was really going to happen, I never heard the word "prepare."

As mentioned, "maneuvers" meant aimless walking around. The officers were lost so often on maneuvers that the regular soldiers had to help them find their way. Even in the unusual case, when I knew where and how to get somewhere we were trying to get to, I offered no suggestions.

My input was not requested, and I frankly didn't care if we did or didn't get to Point Charlie by 0400 hours. All the hours were just about the same. "Hurry up and wait."

I always, always, always had a paperback book with me – whenever or whatever we did. I usually got lots of reading done. I was told "James, just put that f---king book away!" I would do so, and then take it right back out when General Illiterate moved on. I always kept extra books packed in my car for weekend drills, my footlocker when on active duty, and in my backpack.

The sum and substance of our maneuvers was to get sore feet and insect bites.

Lost

One summer camp we flew to Puerto Rico to train. Since this camp involved multiple jumps and some extended nights in the field, we again had some overseas injections to receive. That went fine for a change.

The first jump was a different story. As so often happened, my stick (line of jumpers on the left or right of the aircraft) missed the drop-zone, but I really missed the DZ. I found myself in a large piece of woods, all alone. I saw no other paratroopers, no other planes coming over, and no sign of civilization. I gathered my parachute and hiked to the top of a little hill to look around. Nothing! I saw no sign of others, or even local residents. No sign of life.

"Well," I thought, "no sense in hiking somewhere because I wouldn't even know which direction to head off to." I decided I can't find them, so they will just have to find me – I hope!

I had a little water, but no food. After waiting under a tree at the top of my little hill for about 4 hours, I saw no sign of activity, and decided I'd better prepare to spend the night. I built a small fire since the smoke could help them locate me. I slept on the ground that night and early the next morning I heard some activity in the forest about 100 yards away. I managed to sit up by the time I heard the familiar voice of our Platoon Sergeant "James, I hate to wake you up, but it's time to go."

"Right, sergeant," I said, "got anything to eat?"

Racial Integration

Integration in the U.S. got a tremendous boost from the U.S. military. Overt forms of discrimination were not "allowed," but it happened anyway. In my experience, minority groups usually segregated themselves. The so-called "white majority" was changing in the active-duty military as actual combat roles were over-represented by minority groups, and the officer corps was over-represented by Whites. I'm told, in the current military that has changed significantly. I hope so.

In summer camps I saw much more integration and actual cooperation between racial and ethnic groups. In my National Guard unit, I saw little diversity.

Exception: The greatest diversity in my home unit was the numerous brands of beer consumed.

Overall, in the U.S. Army I experienced, overt discrimination was not allowed; covert discrimination was ignored.

Night Jump

Next to concern over high winds, a parachute that fails to open, or pilots missing the drop zones, a big fear of paratroopers was night jumps. The reason is obvious – you can't see where and when you may or may not land.

We were at the annual two week summer camp of active duty at Ft. Hood, Texas. The preparations were a little more subdued than usual. I sensed a more cautious attitude, especially with the "too many medics" evident at the airfield.

In- flight preparations were normal, but everyone was more anxious than was typical. Exiting into the pitch black was so strange as to be surreal – dreamlike. You could see virtually nothing around you, but you could hear other troopers talking, occasionally yelling and even grunting. With virtually no moonlight, the drop-zone dark, we fell from the sky. Suddenly, without any significant warning the ground seemed to race up to our feet and legs, and smack, we were there. My landing was harder than most, but without injury. Unfortunately, seven in our company were injured, one seriously – a broken back. The army leaders never talked about injuries in jumps, especially night jumps. We grunts did.

Fiery Chinook

The huge Chinook helicopter is capable of transporting up to 30 or more paratroopers, with equipment. I didn't mind so much, comparatively, jumping from the Chinook, because there was little prop blast that could push or spin you around as happens in fixed-wing aircraft, especially the C-141 jet transport.

It was a routine jump as we gained elevation and approached the drop-zone. We felt a mild shudder and then smelled smoke. One of the huge rotor engines was on fire, and belching smoke. On the P.A. we hear our Jumpmaster bellowing "Hard landing men, hang on!" About 30 seconds later we did sort of land and sort of crash, but made it to the drop-zone instead of coming down in the surrounding forest. We were all scrambled together, with equipment scattered everywhere, trying to get unbuckled when two pilots literally climbed over us yelling "Fire! Fire!"

We all did manage to get out without serious injuries. We did smell like smoke and fuel, but no casualties. We were not happy, however, with our "save your own ass" pilots.

Impaired Pilots

How about another pilot story?

We were waiting by the tarmac, preparing to board and jump out of the huge C-141 cargo jets. Swerving down the runway came a Jeep loaded with the pilots for our plane. The driving was erratic, but the jeep made it to our C-141. They tumbled drunkenly from the vehicle and tried to climb the back ramp to the plane.

As a group we all started cursing at these pilots. Our Platoon Sergeant told us to shut up and stand to prepare to board. We did quit yelling but we didn't stand. We sat there until about 30 minutes later, a replacement crew showed up and some MP's escorted the drunken pilots off the plane.

We then, as a group, stood up and began to board.

Injured at Summer Camp

At the two week summer camp of my third year in the National Guard, we had been trucked to Ft. Collins, Colorado. A long trip cramped in the back of a rattle-trap, diesel-smoke-infested obsolete truck.

After settling into the concrete-based outdoor tents we began the usual hurry-up and wait routine so typical. We start preparations for a parachute jump the next day by cleaning, checking equipment and then doing it all over again. Next, many of us spent the rest of the day painting the white rocks surrounding our tents. Why is it, I wondered once again, that the Army so loved small rocks painted bright white on many of their training bases? That and "policing" up cigarette butts on the training fields. We hardly ever found any butts since smoking areas were so tightly regulated with smoked cigarettes put out in little cans painted bright red.

We got up early the next morning (4:30 a.m.) to the sound of banging metal trash cans (another army favorite morning routine). Jump time is scheduled for … Oh, I almost forgot, they don't tell us things like that. Some light exercise followed by gearing up and loading into the trucks to go to the airfield.

I'm getting ready to jump off the back of the truck, and suddenly I'm pushed, hard, from behind. Not jostled as is typical, but pushed. I crash to the ground, injuring my left knee. I'm rolling around in the dirt, loaded with all my equipment on my back,, holding my left knee (which was injured years earlier in a pick-up flag football game). Someone then trips over me as I'm break-dancing on my back in the dirt, and lands hard on my injured knee. Thank you.

Almost immediately I hear a typical question from the platoon sergeant "What the f-ck is the matter with you? Get up we have a jump to make!" I ignore him as I'm taking off my backpack. I then try to stand. I can't. I unlace my jump boots to pull out the tucked in fatigues to examine my knee. By then some medics have arrived, along with a couple officers, one also cleverly asking "What the f-ck is the hold-up here?"

Again, I ignore all this as I'm trying to figure out why my left knee is on fire. One medic pulls out a pair of scissors as he boldly announces "Here let me in here. I'll take care of this." He cuts my fatigue pants leg up to above the knee almost to my groin. To this I do pay attention and say something like "Be careful with those scissors." Corporal Red Cross, offended, says indignantly to me "Hold on there, I'm trained." I could imagine what training a National Guard medic got, but I don't say anything to make it worse – yet. As he is looking at my very rapidly swelling knee, he asks "What the hell happened to you soldier?" Great, another John Wayne weekend warrior who is more like a M.A.S.H. TV character. I couldn't help myself, and say "While I was jumping out the back of this truck here, my left knee was hit by an incoming RPG (rocket-propelled-grenade)." "Very funny wise-ass", he retorts. "I had a bad landing", I say simply, still holding my knee". Look at that f--king knee" he says.

I give up on him as he next says "Are you OK?" "Go away" I said. "Hey, I'm just doing my job here, just like you!" "My God that knee hurts", I say to myself.

I'm loaded into a jeep ambulance and we head out to the closest first-aid station. After a bumpy ride there, I'm helped into a small waiting room. After about an hour an army male medic helps me into an examining room, takes a quick look at the basketball-sized knee and says "Get hurt on a jump?" Yes, I say, jumping out the back of a truck." He thinks this is perhaps the funniest thing anyone ever said and laughs for maybe 5 minutes. I hurt too much to join in the fun. Finally, he says, "Well, I can't do anything for you except give you a couple Tylenol."

"That's a plan," I say. I get the Tylenol, swallow it and he says "OK, now you can go back to your quarters." "Quarters?" I think to myself. Does he think we're on an aircraft carrier here?"

My mind is slowly starting to clear and I say, "I have a problem or two here. One, I can't walk, Two, how do I get back to my 'tent' quarters?" "Oh, that," he says. "You can catch a shuttle bus out front."

So, I'm carried out front to sit on a little green bench to wait for a little green bus to take me back to the tent. As I'm waiting on the bench my medic comes out, sits down next to me and says "Hi. You know, I've been thinking about that knee, and I think you need to go to the base hospital to have it looked at."

"That's a better plan," I say. So he gives me directions about how to take the little green bus to the hospital, and I commence to wait some more.

Eventually, the correct little green bus comes along and the driver helps me on board. Finally, a nice guy. He says "I'm going to take you directly to the hospital. "Thanks", I say.

Next, I'm in the clinic/hospital waiting room, holding my boot in one hand. Eventually, I actually get to see an M.D. I can smell the bourbon as he says "Let's get an x-ray of this." Eventually, that happens, and he returns to my little room and says," I'm going to have you see an orthopedist. You have a problem here."

I'll shorten this odyssey by simple saying I spent 2 ½ days riding around on little green buses, eventually seeing an orthopedic surgeon who glances at the x-rays and says "We need to operate." I stare at him and to his total surprise say to him "Captain, why do we need to do that? Can you show me the x-rays and tell me why you want to operate?" "No", he says, I can't do that?" "Can't do that? What do you mean you can't do that?" I say. "I'm telling you what we need to do, and your job is to just do it," he said. "It's my knee, and if you can't tell me why, my answer is NO, you can't operate," I said.

"OK", he said, and he stood up and left the room. Eventually, a new medic came in and said to me "Well, that went well, didn't it?"

I got a pair of crutches, got out of there, and gimped around the rest of summer camp, doing next to nothing. When I got home, I went to a real orthopedist. I eventually received arthroscopic surgery back at my university hometown hospital.

Chapter 6: Life in the National Guard

Back In the Armory

It was interesting to return to my Texas Air National Guard base in Texas. There was only one other soldier who returned with me, and with whom I trained at Ft. Polk. As mentioned earlier, he was an attorney who was in a similar situation as was I. He had been in law school when his draft notice was being processed. So, I knew one person in our National Guard unit, and we became relatively close friends. We were both happy to be through with the active duty (for now) and back in school.

As described earlier, the schedule in the National Guard called for one weekend per month for training, and a Summer Camp of two weeks duration.

There were few excuses allowed for missing a weekend meeting (hence the derogatory term "weekend warrior" that Regular Army people applied to us). Actually, I didn't mind the term. It was much better than the alternative.

The weekend drills were, overall, boring, punctuated by brief periods of ridiculousness.

Example 1: "Today, we're going to have a refresher class on how to salute" said the Senior Company Sergeant "Everyone in formation. Now!"

Example 2: "Today and tomorrow we're going to be cleaning all the M-1 rifles in the armory. Interesting, since we had trained on active duty with the M-16 which was used in Vietnam, and we are now cleaning obsolete World War II rifles. "Right, now let's take them apart" says our sergeant. I'm thinking "I've never seen one of these, except maybe in a movie." They were heavy, worn-out, and I wondered if any of them would even fire. Doesn't matter. We cleaned these pieces of junk for two days. When we went on the active duty rosters each year for summer camp, we were back to the M-16's. In six years I never saw any of these M-1 rifles fired. Once again, it doesn't matter.

Example 3: This weekend we're going by trucks to Ft. Hood to use their firing range. It's time to re-qualify on the M-16 and 45 pistol. So, we all climb in the "Deuce and a halfs" (2 ½ ton trucks so pervasive in the Army for troop transport). Off we go on our road trip after an hour of sitting in the back of the dusty, cramped truck in the parking lot. We're slowing down. Oops, we're all pulling over to the side of the road – all 24 trucks. Don't even think about asking to get out. After sitting for half an hour, we learn one truck has a flat tire. One fresh lieutenant comes to the back of our truck to tell us "we're not waiting any longer for the repair truck to get here, we're heading out." I'm thinking "that's good to know, let's get on to the next "hurry up and wait project."

After four hours on the road (and side of the road) we arrive at the Ft. Hood firing range. We all pile out of the trucks, get into formation, and march about 100 yards to the entrance of the range.

"Have a seat, men," the officer in charge of the range announces. We do so in the incredibly windy, dusty field. He leaves and about 45 minutes later the range officer struts back to our company (about 120 men) and says "Attention". We all stand up in formation – again. "We're a little short of ammunition today so we can only take six of you to try to quality. Maybe we'll have more ammo tomorrow." The laughing is almost deafening." "Oh, shut up" says the range officer. Some of us do.

After another two hours of sitting in the dust and dirt, our company captain tells us "Attention," and we stand up as then he says "get into formation". Again, we do. He then tells us "our trucks will be here in 10 minutes. We're going back to the Armory." About 1 ½ hours later, the trucks rumble in and we all pile back in to return to the armory. Productive day. The next day we all expect to go to Ft. Hood again. In first formation, our sergeant says "no Ft. Hood today, we don't have the trucks reserved to go again today. Instead, we're going to work on Field Manual 46-11A, How to Prevent Frostbite."

Example 4: "This weekend we're going to work on PT" our Platoon Sergeant says "I think many of you are getting out of shape." That was true. We were. Remember, our "good old boys" loved their beer and most didn't love exercise. "We're going to start with a 3 mile run," he goes on. "Twenty-four laps around the Armory complex is equal to 3 miles, so let's get started." We start running around the armory, and within 10 minutes are so spread out that some soldiers are lapping the slow ones. Within about 30 minutes, no one knows how many laps they've run (or claim they don't) and soon after that, everyone is walking. Probably two of the slowest walkers, much less runners are the Platoon Sergeant (5'6" and 320 +lbs) and the lieutenant recently assigned to our unit. I'm worried about the lieutenant. He was wheezing badly right after we started out. He drops out and disappears somewhere.

Example 5: "Today we're going to have a class on how to repair our Army-issued air mattresses." I should note that almost, if not everyone in our company had given up on these cheap, always deflated air mattresses and bought one of our own. One that really worked. Doesn't matter. We had classes on how to properly inflate, and patch our Army air mattresses. Most of us couldn't even find our defective air mattresses, had to be issued new ones along with a stern lecture about the value and importance of U.S. Government property. I bet the cost of the thin air mattresses to the Army was about $50.00 but worth 29 cents, if that. "If you lose this air mattress again, a letter of reprimand is going in your personnel file," threatens our banty-rooster sergeant. Ok, bill me.

Example 6: (Thankfully, the last example for now) "At attention men" our brave captain shouts. We are going to be viewing some U.S.

Army training films today." (I should mention most of these films were Black and White and dated from World War II and the Korean War). "The first" he droned on " is about personal hygiene in the field, and the second is on anti-submarine warfare. Pay close attention." What?

Tornado

I am not proud of this story. About two years into my service, our unit was called up for active duty by the Governor of Texas to help protect a nearby town that had been damaged by a tornado.

Our assignments involved patrolling the damaged sections of the town, to ensure there was no looting. I thought at the time, "Finally we may do some good."

We were deployed around the town- a small rural Texas community, in groups of 4-6 soldiers in different shifts through the days and nights.

I'll make it quick, because it is painful to recall. There were no incidents, at all, of the citizens of this small town or any other town doing anything unlawful. Sadly, some items disappeared from businesses in the downtown area. Two to three guardsmen showed up with some merchandise – probably, likely, or most assuredly from those businesses. Those businesses needed protection FROM the National Guard. To my shame, I didn't report it to our commanding officer. I tell myself I wasn't physically there when what happened did happen. I didn't see it myself, but… I did nothing.

Vacation in the Dominican Republic

Beautiful beaches, warm weather, welcoming locals – what more could you ask for in a long weekend get-away?

A large segment of the Texas Air National Guard was planning joint military maneuvers and training in conjunction with the Army of the Dominican Republic. Hard to believe, but true.

We flew out of Dallas, planning a combat jump near an airfield on the southern coast of the Dominican Republic. The weather was calm – a good day for a jump, but we did have one big problem. The pilots missed the drop-zone for about half the Battalion. Estimates suggest about 200 men landed in the water. I was one of them. Fortunately, it was fairly shallow – about 4 ft deep. No one drowned, but much equipment was lost. Good start for our training weekend.

The maneuvers with the DR Army started off reasonably well, but the language differences soon emerged as we had few who could speak Spanish and the DR Army had few who could speak English. I saw lots of pointing and other hand gestures, but field coordination of troop movements degenerated into mass confusion. As we moved into the jungle areas the "playing war" became almost comical. I was just glad there was no live ammunition as I heard and saw blanks going off with lots of shouts (in Spanish and English) of "Cease fire! Cease fire!" No one had to tell me that. I was not firing in this confusion anyway.

Someone, presumably in charge of this circus, called off the war games for the day, and we moved off to our encampment location next to the DR soldiers. As it turned out, it was too close.

Somehow, alcohol was available to both armies, and by late night, there were many inebriated men. That's when the fights started. My army had a fairly good number of what one might call "rednecks" who weren't exactly fond of the DR Army , and the rumble accelerated. It took about 90 minutes to get both sides separated, and it seemed the Goodwill Training between nations was threatened.

To no one's surprise, the maneuvers were called off, and we flew home the next day. What a trip!

Diversity

Out National Guard unit consisted of exactly 3 Mexican-Americans, 0 African-Americans and a whole bunch of Texas "good old boys." Roll call at each morning formation where names were individually called out was always intriguing when the sergeant came to the Mexican-American names. I can still remember the three most mispronounced names I had ever heard – and the different combinations of how they were mispronounced. And, across the 5 1/2 years I was there the names were never corrected and pronounced properly. Remarkable.

The names:

Martinez – accent rarely and by accident on the correct syllable.

Garcia – how can you never get this right?

Chirruco – forget it! His name became CHICO.

I am still reminded of these mispronounced names today when I hear them correctly pronounced in conversation on TV or wherever .

Promotion

The U.S. Army makes a big deal about promotions. When you begin your Army experience you are an E-1 (Enlisted Grade 1 – the lowest). If you're still breathing after AIT, you are promoted to E-2 (Enlisted – Grade 2). Some soldiers think they have just won a Gold Medal at the Olympics. Some Army leaders would help support that belief. After Basic and AIT, if you are now still breathing and can stay awake for the ceremony, you may be promoted to E-3 (Enlisted – Grade3). Now you're getting somewhere. Another increase in pay (about $8.50 per month) and much more responsibility. Wash those dishes like the highly skilled soldier you have become.

By the end of my six years total – active duty then five and a half years in the reserves, I was an E-4. I had so much responsibility, I could hardly shoulder the load. I was called a specialist E-4. What I specialized in I never quite understood. A Specialist Army Infantry Airborne foot soldier, I guess. It's funny, I never really felt special.

SHORT

In the military, a frequent discussion involved some endpoint in time for a given deployment, or unit of training, like the end of Basic Training, the end of AIT, or the end of Airborne School. As you got close, you were "short." For example, "I'm short 102 days and a wake-up."

I had 3 months to go in my total 6 years of service, so for me, I was short. In an interesting turn of events, our company commander summoned me to his office during a weekend drill meeting.

He started off the conversation with "I think we're probably wasting our time here James, but I want to talk to you about the possibility of you re-enlisting." "Yes sir," I said. He looked at me questioningly and I couldn't help but smile. Then he said "does that 'yes, sir' mean you will re-enlist? "No, sir," I said. " I thought so," says our peerless captain. "Is there anything I can say or do to get you to change your mind?" Captain Marvel asks. "No, sir," I again said.

"In that case, I want to send you to a school for some more training," says Captain Crunch. Shocked I said, "Sir, I have only 3 months remaining and I'm out of here. Why would you want to send me to school for training?" "I think it would be good for you James. You haven't even heard what type of school it is. Do you want to know?" "No, sir," I said. "I can't believe you don't even want to know what kind of school you could go to," replies our esteemed leader. "Please believe it, sir" I replied.

"I'm going to tell you, since you really want to know, James", he remarks. I must have had a disgusted look on my face, because he calls me to attention. I comply. "The school you're going to is for 6 months, so you will need to re-enlist. It's a school to learn how to do army payroll for our National Guard Unit," he says.

I couldn't help it, and start laughing out loud, almost doubling over in a fit of humor. Our fearless leader doesn't agree it's so funny and this time loudly, yells "Attention!" I barely pull myself together and he yells again "Attention! this is not funny." I'm barely holding on when he of the "I never quit mentality" says, "James do you think this is funny?" I can't help myself at this whole ridiculous meeting and say "Yes, sir." "James," he says, " you're hopeless." "Yes, sir," I say again. Captain Nemo jumps to his feet, pounds a fist on his table, and screaming like a lunatic says "Get out of my f----king office!"

"Yes, sir" I repeat as I leave his office. Has he perhaps, hurt my feelings? I wonder if I should have mentioned that to him.

Later that day, our platoon sergeant took me aside and asked "What did you do to get the Captain so pissed off?" I said, "He wanted me to re-enlist and go to clerk school to learn payroll. I wasn't interested." "You made the right choice there James. We don't need you around here." "That's right sergeant," I said as he, smiling, walked away.

I asked myself for weeks after that "Now why would our loving leader even think of asking me that? He must believe I'm a good soldier. What world has he been living in? Maybe I have him "squared away" now.

Chapter 7: Afterward(s)

Teamwork

The military has a rich history of supporting academic research from social psychologists and sociologists studying teamwork and leadership. On active duty, I saw very high levels of teamwork from the Marines, less so from Army personnel.

Our officers especially stressed the concept of teamwork in talks and classes, but it never really seemed to trickle down. The sergeants, who really run the Army, didn't seem to be pushing that concept: they just told people what to do, and hoped it would get done. Sometimes it worked, but most soldiers I knew felt they were largely "on their own" and were just trying to get through the training – one day at a time.

It was evident to about every soldier I met in the service that the goal of everything we were doing was to go home.

Patriotism

Merriam-Webster defines patriotism as "love for or devotion to one's country."

I am proud and happy to say that I saw this phenomenon in great measure in my time in the military. I saw this in Basic Training, AIT, Airborne School, and in my "Weekend Warrior" status in the Texas Army Air National Guard. I witnessed patriotism in the little things that go on hour by hour like raising the flag, and, similarly, the big things like volunteering for combat duty.

I didn't volunteer to fight in the Vietnam War, but I saw, made friends with, and then lost some of those friends to the carnage. I also lost acquaintances to this horrific mistake. I think it is largely true that old people (politicians) make the decision to go to war, and the young men and women fight and die in the war.

I don't know that this will ever change. I would like to believe it will, but I don't.

Many patriotic young men and women died in Vietnam. Many not-so-patriotic souls also died there. One of the saddest things I saw was patriotism morphed into disillusionment, anger, and hopelessness in the form of depression. As I witnessed this process, I thought so often these young men and women love their country, but their country, our country, doesn't love them in return.

This is how I heard the mission described during my military days:

- Our mission is to kill.
- Our mission is to fight communism.
- Our mission is to kill gooks.
- Our mission is to spread democracy (whether they want it or not).
- Our mission is to honor America.
- Our mission is to stand up for peace (what?).
- Our mission is to show we're the most powerful country on earth.
- Our mission is to save the Godless (by killing them?).
- Our mission is to protect our democracy (By killing people thousands of miles away?).
- Our mission is to protect our country (From invasion by the Vietnamese people on bicycles?).
- Our mission is to do what we are ordered to do (Now this one is really scary).
- Our mission is to do our duty (Who gets to define duty?).
- Our mission is to stand up for our way of life (And force it on others?).
- Our mission is to stand up for what's right (Again, who gets to say what that is?).
- Our mission is to come back alive (I heard this most often from trainers who had been in Vietnam).
- Our mission is to survive another day.
- Our mission is to protect ____ from ______. (Yes, just fill in the blanks).

These mission statements represent, to me, the height of hubris, arrogance, and ignorance.

Good for You!

In spite of all my comments, the military was very good for some people. The young, inexperienced, confused about life and/or career, directionless, and those in or headed for trouble often benefited from the routine and discipline the Army offered.

Not many, but a few received some training that could help them in civilian life. For me, in Infantry training there was little positive carryover, except lots of stories to tell. Some of them even believable and maybe even amusing.

I Was Taught

I was taught:

- To be tough.
- To be a soldier.
- The enemy deserved to die.
- To be stealthy.
- To never give up on a mission (unless I die).
- All Communists are God-hating evil low-lifes.
- To be strong in the face of adversity.
- Not to think, just follow orders.
- Think about what you're doing so you can survive.
- To keep your head down in combat, but attack that enemy (who just
- happens to be shooting at you).
- I am a member of the strongest army in the world (But lost the war in
- Vietnam).
- I am a member of the best trained army in the world (see above).
- God is on our side (see Bob Dylan lyrics).
- We can't lose (see above).

I learned:

- To never volunteer.
- How to look busy.

- How to evade responsibility.
- How to malinger.
- How to say "Yes, sir" when I mean "No, you dumb shit".
- How to subtly complain individually or as a group effort.
- How to march in a parade (badly).
- How to salute.
- How to fall asleep quickly when you are really sleep deprived.
- How to feign enthusiasm (Yes!, Sergeant).
- How to march in ill-fitting army clothing and sweat copiously.
- How to shoot weapons (badly) I would never handle again.
- How to think/not think
- How to wait in endless lines.
- How to appreciate the beauty of OD (olive-drab) green.
- How to tolerate ignorant leadership.
- How to cope with irrationality, short sightedness, and lack of common sense.

The Vietnam War

So many books, so much television, so many movies have been with us since this horrible debacle. Here is a ridiculously simple and brief summary. Multiple sources are annotated by Wikipedia and hundreds of resources provide the following (dates and numbers are always approximate):

Dates:

1 November 1955 – 30 April 1975

(19 years, 5 months, 4 weeks and 1 day)

Location:

South Vietnam, North Vietnam, Cambodia, Laos

Result:

North Vietnamese victory

Withdrawal of American forces from Indochina

South Vietnam is annexed by North Vietnam

Communist governments take power in South Vietnam

Combatants:

South Vietnam, United States, South Korea, Australia, Philippines, New Zealand, Thailand, Khmer Republic, Kingdom of Laos

Supported by:

Spain, Taiwan

VS

North Vietnam, Viet Cong, Khmer Rouge, Pathet Lao.

Supported by:

Soviet Union, China, North Korea, Czechoslovakia, Cuba, Bulgaria

Total dead:

676,585 – 1,035585 Total wounded 1,490,000

Total civilian dead:

1,481,047 – 4,008,047

United States: Total dead:

58,200 Total wounded : 303,644

Effects on the United States:

Loss of life and limb, anger, frustration with U.S. government, division of the citizens, psychological damage to returning veterans, and diminishment of the American belief in invincibility.

Most Important Day in My Life (Almost)

When I graduated from Basic, I was told "This is the most important day of your life."

When I graduated from AIT, I was told "This is the most important day of your life."

When I graduated from Airborne School, I was told "This is the most important day of your life."

When I served my last day in the U.S. Army, I told myself "This is ONE of the most important days in my life."

Afterward

I posed a question on the dedication page of this book. I asked the question, in reference to the Viet Nam war "What did we learn from this?"

I must now try to answer this, from only my perspective. As I watch our foreign intervention in Iraq and Afghanistan, I conclude we have learned little or nothing.

Currently, look at Iraq, Afghanistan and …

John James is a pseudonym chosen to protect the identities of characters described in these stories.

www.ingramcontent.com/pod-product-compliance
Ingram Content Group UK Ltd.
Pitfield, Milton Keynes, MK11 3LW, UK
UKHW040558210726
13854UKWH00008B/1389

9 781304 871442